Pulp E-Mails

A.W. Johnson

DEDICATION

This book is dedicated to our entire family and the stories that live on through all of us

CONTENTS

Pulp E-Mails is a collection of original works

and dialogue compiled in chronological order by date,

from least recent to most recent.

PULP E-MAILS is simply an archive of the vast majority of
email communications between a grandfather and his grandson.
All contents within this book are the actual emails sent verbatim
which have been copied and pasted onto the following pages.
The only omitted content is the author's email addresses.

Any works resembling, or similar to, any other works,

is completely impossible and therefore, is entirely
coincidental thus unintended.

ACKNOWLEDGMENTS

Thanks to all that made Al the man he was:

Linda, baseball, fishing, hunting, billiards, music, Toby's Tavern, jokes, stories, his garden, good bud and bonfires. Most of all, his kids, grandkids and great grandkids. It was family that he truly did love the most.

PREFACE

Like any teenager growing up as new-age technology was exploding out of nowhere every day, I was thoroughly humored when I found out that my Grandpa Al not only had a computer but was on the internet AND knew how to use his email account!

I distinctly recall two defining things at Grandma Linda and Grandpa Al's house: The smell of MacBaren's Navy Flake pipe tobacco, and laughter. I did know for sure that, no matter the time or day, I would jump at the opportunity to go to there. There was something magical about their house - Somebody would always say something that made me laugh, something always smelled good and most importantly, there were always people there. A good chunk of the family was always there. Everyone had a story to tell with a laugh to be shared.

Being a kid in this home was something special. I didn't spend nearly any time at all around Grandpa Al until I was older, at least that I can remember. It wasn't until I was 11 or 12 that I learned his name was Al. I grew up thinking everyone was always saying 'Owl'. Grandpa Owl, that's what I knew him by.

When it was discovered by Grandpa Owl that I was playing guitar and making music, he seemed drawn to me. Nevertheless, I just wanted to become friends. He was my Grandpa and that was a given but I didn't know anything about him. I wanted to start from the ground up.

It just fell into place one day when he invited me into the computer room to hear a song on his computer. Just prior to this, we had been in the living room talking. The late summer sun filled the living room that evening, casting a kind of yellow glow through that giant nicotine stained curtain which hung over a picture window. His vanilla smelling pipe tobacco smoke filled the room despite the front door being wide open and almost the entirety of that side of the family around, going in and out almost constantly. We were in our own world within the happy chaos – My mom, her sisters and their mom cooking in the kitchen, little cousins and new babies running around, in and out of the house and playing the backyard where grandpa's garden was in full bloom; green onions, giant celebrity tomatoes and peas galore. I loved these days more than anything and find myself reflecting back to them every day. Amidst all of this, we had been talking about, 'Dark Side of The Moon, and he said "I have more that you would like." He stood up from the rocking chair as I did from the couch and began to navigate towards the computer room which was at the very end of the hallway beyond the kitchen. That room had been either Tabatha or Teesha's bedroom years before, if I remember right. As we began walking towards that room so he could show me his music, it wouldn't have been right if he didn't begin throwing out jokes and funny insults to everyone around, laughing that hilarious belly laugh that you could hear a block away. Finally, after getting distracted and talking to everyone for 5 minutes or so he said, "Jesus Christ" quit wasting time dammit! Let's go!" He'd laugh and laugh as we walked back down the hall.

He plopped down in his big computer chair and lit up a stick on incense, placing it in a mason jar full of white looking beans. I never even know what incense was until I was older, but I knew I liked the smell. This time, like most others, there was a thick blue glass pipe laying near the keyboard. He realized I was looking at it and jumped – "Who the fuck left this shit back here?!" he would holler while acting so surprised. He'd always place it in a drawer to his right. I never even realized what was going on or why he was saying that. He would go on to put that pipe to use until the day he passed away. I can see it clear as day. I wonder what ever happened to it?

With old Westerns blaring on the TV directly to our left, we sat at the computer desk. He showed me thousands of song titles on his computer and told me he would burn each and every one of them onto discs for me. I now have one disc that says, "A thru Clapton", written in his sloppy handwriting in black sharpie – a mp3 disk with 98 songs.

The next week he showed me, 'A Salty Dog' by Procol Harum. He had many more unbelievable tracks that broadened my musical spectrum of appreciation. He burnt me two disks of, 'The Men They Couldn't Hang', which sat beside his tower for 2 months. I had become very busy with performing and finding excuses to miss class and never went over there to get the disks. One day, I came home from school to find an email in my inbox from him:

"Don't bother trying to come and get them because I sent your discs home with your mother! Little prick!" he wrote. I laughed out loud and shared the email with my mom and dad. That was just his way.. crude yet funny with nothing less than the best of intentions. Always.

Our friendship had started.

I went into the living room and asked Mom about those disks. She told me they were in her purse in a plastic bag. Grandpa Al insisted they be kept in a plastic baggie so they wouldn't end up getting scratched. So, I entered the kitchen and retrieved a plastic zip lock baggie from her purse which contained two navy blue discs. Something smelled strange, though, when I opened the bag to remove the disks. I didn't know what it was.

I looked closer in the bag and found a small bud of weed. It was potent and skunky, not enough to through a party with but enough to make the common man smile. Knowing my grandpa, this was entirely unintentional. And it was.

When I told him he had left some grass in the bag, he howled, laughing so hard he had tears running down his face. The laughing seemed to go on and on. Finally, as he was wiping his tears from his face with the top of his t-shirt, he said, "Awh fuck, I better call your dad!" I was confused but decided not to ask why.

Grandma Linda still shook her head with that smile that only she has and said, out loud, "Oh, Al". I was ten.

Tommy Evans

Sent: Wed 9/30/09 7:51 PM

Here is a voice, do you want to hear more? Knowing that if you do, I am sItting here, with a soul that has been used, abused, and discarded with the same callous way us children were thrown to the world. I have tears running down my face, yet I have a calm inside my skin, because no one knows but me. I kept this shit hidden through all of the therapy that I have done. Some secrets are hidden for life!

number 2

Sent: Wed 9/30/09 7:55 PM

How could it get worse than this?! Where is Dad?

Where is Grandpa and Grandma? What about all of our uncles and aunts?

Who is going to take of us, and how is it my fault? How am I supposed to take care of this?

What is this place? Where is dad going?

..and here I stand with my youngest sister in my arms, my little brother hanging onto my pants and both of my other younger sisters looking at me with the look that only comes out of the eyes of children who do not understand what has happened or know what is about to happen yet, they know nothing will ever be the way it was.

How could Dad just leave us here? Now that was a major question! I had no one to turn too whom I could ask what had happened to us or what I could do about it. Yet, I accepted that it was really up to me; everyone else had either left or never showed up!

So, what in the world was this place? It looked to be beautiful, and yet it held the promise of pain to come.. with manicured lawns and shrubbery, bricks laid straight and in circles, the windows covered in bright green-growing vines, nothing gave an indication that danger was hidden and imminent here!

<u>here is the poem, for me, as yet not re-written</u>

Sent: Wed 9/30/09 8:45 PM

I knew the weight of my secret kept
down deep within my skin
a coward's soul was mine to live
alone without a kin
to face the world as a lie
and yet I knew what not to tell
the horror that lay within
the truth came with my first thought
it was this weight to carry
for being born was all wrong
with no need to linger
but forward I did step
into each moment
alone
afraid
without a choice

Fate placed a finger on my shoulders
for me to carry
mother said my head was big
and would not flush
and through my life I searched
and water was the enemy
used, abused and wasted
before the fruit of life
was tasted
but still I trudged
as a bird -
slowly basted:
served without a thought and
fear as the only condiment

The age of nine with innocence lost
while in the crib
the fault was mine
I could not shake
so forward I marched
beholding my fate
alone in life, alone at night
without a tool too to save myself
the rook did move upon the board
my route was fully twisted

The way to Heaven, from a Priest
lay in the morning misted
too young to know about how to go
and still I feared and treaded
into the light and dark I trudged
not allowing myself to
look for hope,
and still knowing what I dreaded
Allies—little did I know!

My soul was spent by others
who used me at their discretion
the gates of Heaven opened up and
mine was lost
while others drank the gift of life
and I marched on
undaunted

The truth that burned inside my skin
told me what I feared the most - my truth
was,
unwanted

At times I dawdled but still I trudged
not knowing where safety was
for whom I turned to, cast me off

as if I was the liability
too young and soft, too young to die
the task that lay ahead was
to be and stay alive, and,
laugh at them instead

But truths as this came hard on me
too much for me to carry
too small and young
to know when to run

The danger lay where safety was
with family and predators..
what was the difference?
 I could not tell,
yet still I stroked for distant skies,
not seeing sanctuary or solid shores

then came the time
when I was laid into the dark
four generations
of children mourned
no longer could they feel
the comfort of my smile
and still I crawled each inch of my miles
"Fuck you," I laughed,
as this was my only style

<u>save this one</u>
Sent: Mon 10/05/09 4:42 PM

I went into the piss hole to brush my teeth and get ready for school. I always tried to be first so I would not be a vulnerable target when Jimmy the Jap got up. My eyes were still showing a light cast of darkness above my cheeks and my nose would not heal straight, that was for sure! As I looked into the mirror, I made myself a promise: if the Jimmy the Jap bothered me again, the next new kid that came into this piss hole was going to be my pigeon. Whoever that poor fucking kid was, he was going to suffer a stiffer row to hoe than the path that lead me. Just one more fucking time and Jimmy the Jap was gonna get his!

I finished brushing and Bobby came in and picked up my toothbrush as soon as it hit the holder. It was one of those funny looking things that is supposed to hold a cup and six toothbrushes.

"What are you doing?" I asked.

"I am going to fix that fucking slant-eyed cocksucker! Watch!" he said as he dropped his pants and ran my toothbrush around and up and down his ass crack,

"That is my toothbrush, Goddamn it! Jimmy's is that blue one over there!" I yelled as I pointed to the next sink

"How fucking long have you been doing this? Goddamn! Goddamn!"

" A couple of months," he replied. And then I puked.

Secrets
Sent: Sat 10/17/09 8:24 PM

The first day of first grade finally arrived and I liked it! There was recess, lunch, another recess, and then it was back home.

Sometime later into the school year as we got into arithmetic, the teacher had an idea and she put a fraction up on the blackboard. And I got it!

This was something that I became really interested in; the bottom number turned the top number into pieces! It was like cutting a pie! Well, cutting a pie the way mom did, because I wasn't allowed a sharp anything yet. Someone had been watching me.

When school was done for the day, my teacher walked back to my desk and handed me an envelope as she said, "I want you to take this home with you and give it to your Mother." And I did. My Mother had a wooden spoon that was made out of the kind of wood used to make baseball bats or some other kind of hard wood which would have sufficed in rendering Frankenstein helpless. It was about three feet long. She used this wooden club to do the laundry. She would stir the clothes with it and when she rinsed them in the hot water she used it. She would dip it into the old white washing machine with the wringer on top of it and pick out clothes one by one to run through the wringer.

Now, being young, I did not see what was coming and my ass exploded! Holy shit! She swung that fucking spoon like a samurai swing a sword! I took a beating!

I was bawling and screaming

"No! What'd I do?" I yelled as the whapping continued and when the beating was over, Mom was screaming at me things I couldn't understand. Out of part of the garbled yelling came the words kind of like,

"Draw nasty pictures on your school papers and embarrass me!" As the beating continued.

I had no idea what I was getting a beating for and I had gotten enough of them to know that I did not want the next one, no matter what! Everything inside my digestive system turned to water. I tried to understand what had just happened to me and I had no idea what was going on. Later in the night, as everyone was asleep and the silence belonged only to me, I went over my school papers as warm tears ran while my head seemed to pound and pound from all my crying. Nothing. I just couldn't figure out what I had so wrong. Nothing!

Recess was a real lot of fun for me. I could play with other children and the two twin brothers who would ask me over to their house to watch Red Ryder and Gene Autry on their television set! They were the first family in Sweet Water, Montana to own a T.V set.

In school we had done the Golden Rule until it was like second nature, so there was no conflict during recess. After all, this was the only place that I felt sanctuary. This was the place where I did not feel fear.

A few days later as the teacher started to talk about fractions, I started doodling on the top of my math test. I drew a circle and started to divide it by drawing lines through the round ring.

I got up to making sixteen parts of the top number and that is where I ran out of space because my pencil made such a wide line. Just before the go home bell rang, my teacher marched down the middle isle to my desk and handed me a sealed envelope as she said, "Take this home and give it to your Mother!"

"Fuck you!" I thought.

"Yes Ma'am." I said politely "Will give it to her as soon as I get home!"

I threw that fucking thing into the first garbage can I came to as I walked the fourteen blocks to the apartment we lived in.

For the next week, my teacher wanted to know if I gave that envelope to my mother.

I lied. After a week or two, my teacher left the class room about an hour before school was finished for the day. We had some substitute teacher take her place, and finally, school was done for the day. My heart stopped as I opened my home's door and there stood my mother and coldhearted I looked over and seen my teacher. "Her!" I thought. The look in my mother's eyes told me that I was in deep shit again and truly, right down to the bottom of my soul, I had no idea why I was going to get to see the wooden spoon again. Mom's face had that look, the look that let me know that no matter what I was not going to invite another friend, kid, or someone I just met into my home! I was not going to like what was about to happen!

"Thank you, Mrs. Ryder, I hope this will end this problem!"

My guts turned to water!

I did recognize a battle field and I was going to get a beating. "What in the hell was going on? I kept asking myself as I tried to understand why I had stepped into something where only I would pay a price for admission and everyone else knew! They had a game plan and Mother was an expert at dealing out a whomping with that wooden spoon for my minor and unknown indiscretions. The beating took place and I promised that whatever it was I had done, I would never do it again! I promised there would be no more letters from Miss traitor, and still the beating continued!

The next week during recess, I sat on the soft-seated swing. I tried to walk as if nothing was wrong. I walked slow, but I did not limp. That next Friday, when I opened our home's door, I knew I was going to be a long weekend. Her and my dad were fighting again and it was brutal. Neither me or my sisters would leave our bedroom to go to the bathroom because the breaking furniture, the screaming, the punching and the words that came out their mouths was frightening. I heard things that would haunt me my whole life! And it was my fault! Whatever had happened, whatever had caused this, the only thing that came through was it was my fault. My head was too big to flush! My birth had been the curse of all of us. Jail was better than being around me as I was the Antichrist, whatever that meant. But I did interpret it as, wow, it really is my fault! I had no idea, but I was not going to open our bedroom door and walk through that war so I could go and pee. I went over and I peed through our bedroom window and it ran around the rock and grass outside.

This would come back to bite me, but, it would almost be a year until that happened which was fine with me, I just wanted to survive now without

t peeing my pants.

I went to the store for my Mom as she was beat to shit with black eyes. She went to her syringe and she was low of medicine. I did this for two weeks, and at school, I was scared that someone would figure out what was happening at my home. Sure as shit, my teacher handed me another envelope that was sealed, and told me to take that to my Mother. Oh yea, I was gonna do that as soon as I could get that chore done! I threw the fucker before I left the school. Again, I lied when she asked if I had given that letter to my Mom and some of the stuff I lied about even amazed me! I did not matter.

Along came Wednesday and my traitor was at my home when I got there. The beating commenced as soon as she left.

"Draw nasty pictures on your papers!" Oh, the beating was severe!

I pleaded and I begged and I swore I had no idea about what they were talking about and why I was getting tuned up again and then my Mother showed me my math paper and there was the circle that I had dissected as I comprehended a very small and very neat rule of mathematics.

I guess my pie charts did resemble a woman's anatomy in her eyes. I still shake my head today.

another part of a book, or another book , or just another chapter

Sent: Sat 10/17/09 6:47 PM

  The trip had been a hard trip. Nothing came easy and nothing was what I expected. I knew by now that I would have to find my spot in the 'pecking order'. I stopped at the main door for the orphanage in Idaho. It had taken me three weeks to get here by bus. If you are young, and you have to go to a new place, do not do it by bus. I swung my two grocery bags with the string handles that held all that I owned against the doors and they opened. I immediately saw that I was expected; there were about ten kids staring at me and all of their looks told me that now was the time to choose if this was going to be OK, or I was about to get my ass kicked! Sure enough, here he came, a heavy set kid who was Indian and I almost wanted to laugh about it since I was coming from and Indian Mission full of Nuns and Indians.

The pedophile 'house father' said to the fat kid coming at me, "Well Junior, you better do good or you know what is going to happen tonight!"

  I saw fear in the kid's face. I did not know what the faggot bastard meant but I understood the unspoken threat! The fat kid did too! As I let loose of the string handles of my two sacks of my stuff which was one well used tooth brush, two pair of shorts and one blue flannel shirt with black lines that made the shirt plaid, I hit the fat kid full in the nose and mouth. He went down like a ton of shit!

Kawhomp! And then he pissed his pants. His eyeballs were rolled back up into his head, and he was out!

Oh yeah, this was gonna be a fun place to survive in! Now the House father looked over to Jimmy the Jap and said, "Well, are you going to let him beat your new lover up?"

I had no chance. I had both eyes blackened, both upper and lower lips were split open and I think I had two broken ribs when the Jimmy the Jap finally ran out of wind.

To me, it was a mild beating, nothing like what I had experienced before. My nose was bleeding and as I picked up my two brown paper bags of my stuff, the house father hit me in the back of my head and my whole world went black.

It took a few moments for me to try to understand what the hell had just happened to me and none of it made sense. I tried to gain some kind of understanding of why did I hurt so much and how was I supposed to deal with this?

<u>a poem for granola</u>

Sent: Mon 10/19/09 9:46 PM

I rolled a pinner

that's all I had,

wanted one more

but,

that's all I had.

As good as it is,

it was way too bad.

Why don't you help me,

you limp dicked lad?

Don't take

give

 to the old man!

Hahahaha!

Cheap cocksucker!

Give to the granola

when I am done;

A respect is what

cost one!

another chapter--think about this, let me know?!?!

Sent: Mon 10/19/09 11:09 PM

I was 12 when Dad forced me to write a letter to Grandma in Sand Cooley, Wyoming.

My oldest uncle was the elder of four brothers and three sisters and he believed in the oldest being cherished! No matter what, all was his and he looked at me as if I was the Anti-Christ!

He was a full colonel in the VFW. He was the god boss of every parade and absolutely the rightful owner of all that had been accrued through his time.

When he looked at me at any dinner, or, for most of you, noon meal, he never past up an opportunity to let me know that all of them thought of me as shit. If they didn't, he would change their mind and I paid the price for this. For me, I thought of myself as if I was on a crusade; A piece of shit that was trying to redeem myself by going on a Holy Crusade! No matter what he said, I was only responsible in his eyes. So, my crusade was a failure even before I started. By then, I had made up my mind that I would look at him and the rest of them at the table during Sunday dinner after Church, and not show any emotion. His words cut to the core of my being, and even though I was only twelve years old, I promised myself that I would not give him, or the rest of the people who were supposed to take care of me, any satisfaction!

Of course this was immature and self-serving but I had no other tools of survival to fall back on.

The brutal truth was way too hard to ingest, or to think about - and that left me all kinds of truths to use to protect, none of which had to have anything to do with reality.

All of them looked at me, and they placed on my shoulders all the shit and finger pointing because they had no one else to hate for the loss of their sister or their daughter or even their hate for themselves which they could not acknowledge.

So here I came, and I had different criteria for each one of them and I swore to myself that I would not let any one of them see that the words thrown at me were just as deadly as any weapon a killer would use to end the life of their innocent victim.

   Sunday after Sunday, I heard all of his words just like I was listening to a TV show and to me, it did not matter. I soon grew a very thick skin. A skin that I wonder if you would have the fortitude to endure? Of course I thought to myself, "This is not what a young child is supposed to deal with." But nor was the dice of life thrown for me and my younger siblings.

I need positive re-enforcement, and this is more bullshit, think about it

Sent: Fri 10/23/09 11:26 PM

"Shit!" I said to myself. My escape from the dungeons of youth was still the same; wait until all were asleep, go out the window above my bed, carefully, and step far away until my foot hit the safety railing of the set of steps going downstairs were Archy slept. The same fucking bed that Jimmy the Jap had slept in! He fucked himself, and I had helped that along!

But I was surprised as I walked down the street and down towards all that was supposed to be right. It was dark, and only a forlorn street light showed the darkness with rays of hope and light. I had at least 20 blocks to travel until opportunities for my weaknesses kicked in! I was looking for anything that would, in my mind, transport me to another land, another time, and of course, another set of living circumstances!

I was living an honest to --no bullshit-- adventure!!

I was eleven, no one gave a rat's ass whether I was alive, sleeping or dead! No one cared, and for me, if I didn't do something stupid, like getting caught like I got caught last month, I could wander through the darkness, not disturbing anyone or any fucking barking dog, and I could go with complete immunity! It was perfect! I was not locked into the place where I was not safe! And, no one would come to my bed and use me badly! Here in the dark, I had safety.. darkness.. where no one could question what was I doing, what was I thinking, what did I think I was doing?

I looked up into the darkness and it was broken up with a tapestry that looked like a bunch of little bastards like me had shot at the darkness and poked holes into the protective blanket with B-B guns. I looked at the night and I gave a sigh of relief. It really was as Carl Sagan, years later had said, "Billions and billions of stars," and I felt so insignificant, worthless, used and abused, and still, it was OK. Of course I had only me to protect me and for me, this was it should be; what kind of a story or hero could I strive to be? I giggled to myself as I sat turned into an alley. An alley is a good place to travel at night, from one place to another, especially if you had no destination. Most people show one side of themselves to the street or avenue, but if you come down the alleys in the daytime, you can get another shot at understanding the family, or of the busted up family, and of course, the real fakes of the "real" world.

In the front yard, all was trimmed, groomed, and of course, neat and expected! In the back yard, you could see that the grass had not been cut for a long, long time!

All kinds of shit in the garbage cans; whiskey bottles by the gross! But there was also Gin bottles and in some, there were Vodka bottles! But what I was looking for in the daylight was soda bottles. They paid a nickel! I was overwhelmed by what a nickel could buy!

To me, a nickel could feed me for a day. If I knew that was all the budget could provide for me, it would do! This last summer had been one of the best summers I had ever had. I could get out of harm's way for an entire weekend! I could eat like a king, piss when I wanted to piss and still nurture myself at the rivers-- and I had two to choose from either the Snake or the Clearwater!

I could get matches at any grocery store, they were given freely! For about forty cents, I could get three weenies at the meat counter and a loaf of fresh bread that would just melt in your mouth because of the it's freshness. And that smell took me to a time a long time ago, when I was too young and stupid to know how good that time was, compared to the shit-time I lived in now. And if I had gotten lucky in the daylight hours, I could feed myself and have the time of my life where all I had to do was take care of me.

The river sang a sound of soothing, something like when a mother softly hums a tiny song to her baby.

It was soft, steady, and constantly changing like life. It soothed my soul, and it spoke to the part of me that I wanted to live in all the time. It was sweet, steady, and it was always there, the kind of way that parents are expected to be there.

But now all I gave myself was about another hour and I would have to get back to the shit hole I had to survive in. So I wandered down alleys, where the street lights did not outline me to the black and whites or some fat fucking cop who needed an abandoned kid so he would have a reason to validate his piss-poor understanding of what freedom was - an asshole who needed me! Just like that fucking Archy! A bull queer, no matter what, takes by being mean, tough, and hopefully for itself, valuable in his own world. Well that son of a bitch was gonna get his, just like Jimmy the Jap got his. But, I couldn't think about that now: this special time for me was way too valuable to me to let that piece of shit predator intrude!

I thought about what time of year it was, and school would be starting in a couple of weeks. Jesus! What grade would I be in this year? Who cared? How the hell would I do this?

"Fuck!' I said to myself, as the knowledge that I was another year older and I could not remember what my last birthday had been like, or when, and who had cared ran across. I stopped, and stood there in the dark and thought when was my last birthday that had been acknowledged? "Holy shit!" It has been three years since I had someone who showed that I was alive, and that possibly, I had worth! Now there is a bitter chunk of truth for a child to ingest.

Now all I had to do was go back into the 'jaws of death', forget all that I had thought about this night and still survive, not matter what! Fuck 'em!! They could not continue to do to me what they have done to me forever! I would kill each one of them, one at a time. Or, they would stop, go somewhere else, and if I ever run into one of them there would be an unsolved murder! Just think about this, how many unsolved murders are there in the United States that go unsolved for decades, if they ever get solved??

Yea, there are a lot of dead motherfuckers who deserved to be dead that are dead. Their whole world should give me a parade or 'atta boy', or just name an amount of money, and as *Pink Floyd* said in '*The Division Bell*'... "please go fuck yourself!"

the watermelon

Sent: Sat 10/24/09 2:46 AM

It was a great day with the sun shining in August. The skies were clear and blue without a cloud in sight. Gary and I went down the hill from the 'pit of shit', as we called it, at 21st street and 21st avenue. We were looking forward to the cooling caress of the swimming pool which was a long stretch of road away. We had free passes from the orphanage which they hated handing out to us because it benefited the swimming pool, something about taxes and tax breaks. Though the headmaster and every other adult at the 'pit of shit' tried to fill us with fear and made attempts to make us feel like we were rotten and worthless little rags, we still held those little blue tickets as a token of admittance into a carefree wonderland.

We were telling truths and the normal novelties us kids talked about as we rode our bicycles on a free coast, downhill, all the way to the swimming pool.

"Do you know what I miss the most from being here in this shit hole?" I said to Gary.

"No, what?" he asked.

"When I was small", I began, "And we got to go to my grandfather's farm, as a treat, we would have an ice cold watermelon!" My throat swelled as memories of ordinary life away from this 'pit of shit' and before dad ran away rushed into my head. I wisped in a belly full of air and quickly reverted to my original thought process.

28

"Grampa was always so nice. The taste and smell, even the color of a watermelon takes me back to my earliest memories and the only place I didn't have to sleep with one eye open." I stated in monotone.

"Well, let's go get one!" Gary said.
"Hell, I know where there a lot of watermelons!"

"What are you talking about, I don't have any money to buy a fucking watermelon, you fucking idiot!" I snapped.

"We are gonna steal one!" He replied with a grin. And I smiled. I was in for this!

As we continued to coasted down the long hill to the swimming pool, Gary said,

"Just stay with me and I will show you."

We made a right turn, and went down town to a grocery store that had two big wooden boxes on wheels that must have held 300 watermelons. They were out in the dirt in front of the store, kind of an attraction that was too big to ignore. We went down a dirt alleyway on the side of the old brick store, puffing up dust with our tires. Of course we went right up to the side of the old brick store and leaned out bicycles up against the wall. Gary kneeled down, looking straight at the toe of his hi-tops, resting his chin on his left knee and grabbed the filthy bill of his old dark green baseball cap. He lifted it barely off his head and placed it back down firmly, then retied his shoe, double knotting it at the end.

I stood over him, my shadow cast over his shoe. I said,

"We have to have some kind of plan. We can't just walk up there and steal a watermelon!"

Over the next hour we told each other stories of what we had heard, or made up about stealing watermelons, emphasizing on the one about the farmer shooting someone in the ass with rock salt through a double barrel shotgun.

"How are we gonna know which one to get?" I asked.

"Shit, who cares?" Gary stated hopelessly. "Just get one! You pussy"

"No, that won't work, we'll get caught! And I don't wanna get taken back to the headmaster by the police! I heard my old man say once that you could tell which one was good by thumping on it with your knuckles." I said. We stood there looking over toward the wooden crates. Sure as shit! There they were! Promising cool relief, sweet tasting, and almost begging to be stolen!

 So we walked up to the big bin and started to thump on each melon, trying to find the "good one", and eventually Gary said,

"This one!" I walked over to him calmly with my hands in my pockets of my blue high watered coveralls, and with a mere glance at that glorious melon, nodded in agreement.

He leaned closer to me, looked over his shoulder, and asked under his breath,

"So how do you think we should steal it?"

Having planned this part when we first rode up, secretively and confidently I replied,
"You set it up here on the corner of the bin, and then I'll just

ride my bike past it and as I go by, I'll reach over and grab it and just ride off! It is a done deal! And once I've got it, you hop one your bike and we'll go enjoy our feast on the pool side!"

My heart was pounding. I couldn't believe how perfect of a plan we I had formulated.

I walked back around the corner were we had leaned our bicycles up against the wall, and I started out. Nothing was in my way. I made about six full stroked power pedals of the bicycle gaining a solid speed and as I came by the bin, I reached out with both hands and I grabbed that watermelon!

"I did it!" I thought for a quarter of a second.

I might as well have grabbed ahold of a telephone pole! There was absolutely no give in the melon, I went down like a ton of shit! My plan was shattered in an instant. I just sat there on the sidewalk for a second. I had blood running from many places on my elbows, knees, and my nose. I came up crying , which did not put me a place of admiration with Gary. There were two old ladies that came running to my aid, and they wanted to know if there was anything they could do? Fuck no! So I got up off of the sidewalk, rubbed my burning knees, walked over the god damn bin full of watermelons and picked the fucking thing up and then I just walked down the street to the corner of the block, then made a fast right turn.

I kept walking, bawling like a little girl, and bleeding like a butched hog. It wasn't long until Gary caught up to me on his bicycle, rambling on like a puppy on coffee, reminding me that I left my bike behind and how the headmaster was gonna kill us. With many tears in my eye and blood on my elbow and a face of pure disgust, I ensured him that I didn't give on single flying fuck about either of them and we commenced our afternoon August journey to our carefree wonderland.

(No Subject)

Sent: Sat 10/24/09 5:20 PM

Too easy for me to live with fear

that turned my guts to water

a constant companion of no worth

with nothing left to barter

to feel the fear and touch the fear

was a bitter pill to swallow

but knowing that no matter what

I was not wanted here

so life rolled the dice and

no matter what

they made sure I paid that price!

The ones who should look after me

Instead, the war of words I dodged

but no matter how hard I turned

their venom still hit and lodged!

The safest place for me to be

was by myself

and never would I tell,

but what they saw

did bother me and

sped me on my way

into the Gates of Hell

the home where I would stay!

They turned me here and turned me there

and I ended up all twisted.

So down the road I drifted

not knowing who to trust

and seeing who was gifted!

My truth was to eat a bitter pill

softer than a beat'n.

hunger was familiar,

with nothing left for eat'n!

To never go into the hole

that was the center of my soul,

for safety lay with me when

I was alone!

how could I live

until I would be grown?

ALONE how do you like this one!??

Sent: Sun 10/25/09 2:31 PM

Being alone is a terrible thing,

with great risks

with a horrible sting.

No one to hold me,

no one to please,

no one to help me

no one to sing when the dark is here and steadily creeps.

No one to lean on

and offer comfort

before my sleeps.

When the black covers

that I'm alone,

and fear settles in

to the marrow of the bone.

Alone leaves a bitter taste

and teaches who is only waste

when terror is hidden

with no place to hide

only anger, not sanctuary -

inside mad-dog mean

or to bounce along and

stay contrary!

To veer away from the easy path,

to walk away from jealous wrath.

Only to look down at the dusty tracks

of going through from now

away from the past.

Tomorrow holds empty light,

that may not come.

And, if I piss on my own shoes,

tis only me, not someone else

who does lose!

Being alone has great Freedom,

a chance to live in my own kingdom,

which rests between my ears -

and if I cry

with silent tears,

find no one to belittle

my tiny sighs!

But how do I do this,

staying alive?

No one to walk with

as I strive,

 to hide the hurt,

that pounds inside my shirt?

A birthday comes and goes..

no cake, no gift.

No one seen

can I stay alive until thirteen?

Will I sleep without a dream

or will the morning bring a ray

of hope? Or, will I dance

on the Hangman's rope?

Maybe it's in this instant that I will lie

and have this be all that I give

to me.

Alone?

aww
Sent: Tue 10/27/09 3:42 PM

Hold me close,

to your heart,

as I do you.

Tomorrow bring us colors,

Of pink or Blue?!

To bring us joy,

or bring us grief,

and think of us

as other do.

Family lives on

as the ittie bitties do

the way I love all of mine;

grandkids,

all of the heard,

and you.

scars
Sent: Mon 11/02/09 9:37 PM

To take a child young and prime

and damage him every time,

to feed your arrogance and make

him feel your own slime!

An Altar boy you need to nudge,

and a Priest is there to pack his fudge!

Then ridicule him for just being.

Disregard what he is seeing!

A hidden blow with words,

cuts the deepest,

the same as shit from

the birds!

Of cuts to the soul,

and making sure

of every word he heard!

Oh how powerful, to be God

in this child's world!

and so he comes to feel

the cut of words,

and scars that never heal!

For the child of ten,

to stand and wonder,

when, help would come,

from even thunder?

It is now what is said,

but how it comes across,

a mighty blow, no one knows

and the child feels the loss!

When hope is never there,

but tomorrow says,

a promise of a thought,

is more valuable when ot bought!

Nothing free comes his way,

and no one there to stand and say,

he marches to a different beat,

take that out of him

on his seat,

a wicked blow of words,

with no defense,

tells the god

he has no sense!

Words of ridicule, and

displeasure,

keep the child

from his treasure!

To sit there at the Sunday dinner,

and take blow after blow, word and

word, and of course,

he is the sinner!

Poker faced and still he sat

when they looked at him,

it was his father they did curse,

and he was next, first!

To get the blows they

wanted sent,

Flail away at the

boy sent,

he lied to be here

and now he pays,

by suffering the scars

that will stay!

He felt the words

and he was not bored,

felt the cut as

a samurai,

swinging a sword!

And so he lived as

he was shown,

the scars were deep,

and troubled him,

in his sleep!

No peace was his to steal,

the scars that never heal!

When words should come

from those who hold

this heart so tender,

what can he do except

surrender!

But onward he did step,

wishing only for the peace

that came to him and only

when he sleeps!

The morning new will bring,

the hope of another spring,

not proven false, nor untrue,

and he dedicates himself

anew!

To walk past the words of steel,

and live with the scars,

that never heal!

A target free and clear,

no defense, no one to

hold dear!

Alone at night, alone

in day,

The scars are deep,

and they stay!

No matter what,

without a strut,

he walks alone -

No secrets will he tell,

he lives in Hell!

He never asked for a deal

<u>some more--I bet you did not see this one coming!! haha</u>
Sent: Mon 11/02/09 9:52 PM

One more thing I need to say

about those cocksuckers,

I've outlived all of those

selfish Mother fuckers!

if you don't get a giggle,

you are dead and can

not wiggle!

aww! I bet you did not see this coming!! Sunday Punch with
Vengeance!
Sent: Mon 11/02/09 10:20 PM

I can't believe that your French fries

kept you from seeing the

wonderment of my words!

I slammed my dick in the door,

and fed the raven birds!

Now it's said that I am wrong,

but you know that you,

from me,

are strong!

An outlet rarely seen,

will give relief and

seldom,

the pain of what is not clean.

But, take your solace from

a queen,

mother good

and mother mean

and now,

I am not a being!

A thought slowly steals

from the wounds

that will not heal!

Re: take a peek
Sent: Mon 11/02/09 11:48 PM

I live on with the words we share,

you will tell your great grandchildren

that I was truly a soul bared,

and shared with one vision!

I only want to live to talk with

your great, great itty bitties,

and watch as they discover the

words that tear our soul, or

help us build our cities!

For as I go into the ground,

my life was not wasted,

I live on as each one of

the children have tasted,

all I've tried to be, I've been,

and all I've wasted.

Life is so precious to live

our soul is proud to give

what our lives are..

were to provide you

hope when you needed

to live!

I was stoned and yet I gave

to all who stood their ground,

and disregarded my own grave,

for their path that they have found!

And when you think of me,

my job was easily done,

and if you find you have

a daughter or a son,

teach them to have a

star, and undaunted,

march on!

My whole purpose has been

to come to their aid,

even when taunted!

For they have in their veins, the

strength of Saints, and

those of us flaunted!

The truth be that they are

all that we were!

And, only then will they see

how bright their own star!

My whole purpose in this world

was to touch one who follows,

and on his shoulders, greatly taken,

was joy

and not sorrow!

more shit from Elk Owl

Sent: Tue 11/03/09 6:06 PM

Christmas came and I did sit on the stairs

that led up to my place to sleep.

I had one envelope.

My baby brother had a ton of stuff

that looked like the

toy display in the catalog magazine.

I told myself, they would not

see me weep.

Hide it well and hide it deep,

let them be whom who cannot sleep!

The look that Grandmother gave,

would send a Saint to the grave,

as satisfaction and venom dripped

from a simple glance -

let them not have me

make a stance!

My brother small and young

deserved all he got,

with love lavished on him

always bought!

A thread of truth runs through me,

even if I lied,

before a gift to me was given,

they'd rather I die!

Satisfaction would not come to those,

who harbored thoughts of harm,

for was not me they chose,

but twas my own father!

The price he should have paid,

laid heavy on my shoulders

and to a child the weight was heavy

just like boulders!

I smiled a look of joy when baby brother

opened another toy,

wading through his presents,

let them not find joy by having me

come through bent!

She should have thought that what she'd done,

would not go on forever.

The money to the Church she spent,

would one day

my bladder vent,

with thoughts of never,

brighten her sleep in darkness:

without spring weather!

No rain to fall

no spring to come,

a price to pay

for what she'd done!

And I slept the sleep of the dead,

my baby brother never said

he's seen the truth inside his head.

Satisfaction never seen

from my look of pleasure

she thought that she had

the full worth of her own treasure!

She missed the point of what it meant,

with joy I showed my look well spent

For baby brother, did not deserve

nor could he swerve

away from those

who should care

and cut my heart,

open bare!

Poker faced, I did not look,

for they're the ones who lost the gift,

just like I was in a book,

not the one who's heart is split!

An Altar boy who did God's work,

just in case he did lurk,

but without a tool

and danger at my school!

No one must see

what I tell,

I am living in a living Hell!

A wizard not am I to tell,

but who knows,

'the tolling of the bell',

will bring those to his grave

and think of what to sell.

His heart and soul,

they had to hold,

but shit was all they saved!

Nothing of what I was,

did they see or protect -

only the ruined soul

of a life well spent!

Approval would never come

from what I did

or what I've done;

An Altar boy who did God's work,

and for what they wanted,

I still marched on undaunted!

<u>your mail box is full</u>

Sent: Tue 11/03/09 6:30 PM

You have no idea

how pissed off I am

when I want to talk with you

or make a plan,

but you won't let me!

I sent some shit to you,

and I want to talk,

but as always, you won't change,

and now you won't know

what it is

I want to tell! So,

fuck you! Go to hell!

Slam your dick in the door

like a one dollar whore!

But do not fear:

I am close,

but never near!

<u>an innovation</u>

Sent: Tue 11/03/09 8:59 PM

I rolled a pinner,

that's all I had

wanted another,

but that was all I had.

Gained respect,

lost my sense,

and shot that

yipping motherfucker

through the fence!

shit we've done and how to fix it

Sent: Tue 11/03/09 10:56 PM

"What should I do and can you help me?"

These are words I've used all my life

I stand tall and pay that price

She came clean and innocent,

Not fair to her, as she did give

the words of how to live.

A child hurt, a child given,

her life had met its goal

and that is something I will not

shatter for the solace

of my soul.

The price paid, the price sold,

I was wrong

she was the cost -

Now I know the price

of my own soul.

Credibility? All is lost!

She has the soul of God,

one who could give

more of herself than expected!

She did not need to feel

my own inadequacies,

I fucked with one

of her own strengths

and will pay for them

with my own flaws!

All I've done was
wrong!

Not another word can she see

from you ,

or me!

Now we need an agent!

And legal representation!

because I have fucked us all!

<u>you missed out!! -- an odyssey</u>

Sent: Thu 11/05/09 5:09 PM

"Fuck it!! Just Fuck it!!"""

So I rolled a pinner,

and this I must taste.

GG called that

it was ready, dinner-

some kind of cabbage-

shit that would be ready, when?

"Tastes Like Chicken! Got any 'white sauce?" the Indians ask.

So you missed out on the pinner-

guaranteed to turn any gain

into a loss!

A taste or two,

talk to Jesus!

Another taste,

he talks to you!

This, you could of had,

but your mail box is full

Since it's not me, you want to

talk too!

You are wondering what

you missed out on,

and what you should do is

empty the fucking mailbox

so I may leave

a voicemail.

Fucked up and drunk,

this you won't see,

It can rot until

it smells like a skunk!

When you want

to hear from me,

make it possible where

you can see

the shit I want to show

to you. By emptying your fucking mailbox!

Just like I said,

"I had me a pinner!"

Wish you were here,

so I could slap your

hand, spill your beer!

And if you were here,

I'd whack you with a stick

right where you pee-

You would empty your

mailbox, then you

would see!

The words that pass

from me to you,

is like piss in the wind,

you don't know what

each drop will do;

could be from the heart

or out of the ass,

but if I can't reach you,

I've done all I can.

Oh yea, except leave a voicemail!

spider

Sent: Thu 11/05/09 8:12 PM

On the teeter totter, she sat,

I knelt down by her feet,

on the bottom of her fingers

I did touch and

melted into her dark eyes.

None of this did I deserve

but I knew what I was missing!

You deserve better than me, and

I am unworthy.

Not a movie, or a dance

can I take you too.

I am weak, and

nothing more can

I say!

<u>here ya go</u>

Sent: Thu 11/05/09 9:27 PM

When I can think of romance,

it will be you that haunts me,

for what you deserve, is

a lot more than anything

I can hope to be;

I have no one who cares

if I am dead or alive!

On me you waste your heart

and hope,

for the path that I have to walk,

is steep and on a treacherous

slope.

All I can do is not step into

another trap, you need better

than me but one day you

will surely have your arms

around me, wrapped.

I live where I am not wanted,

and you should not be,

the tool or the weapon,

that brings me or you

into a light that we cannot see.

Sweet dreams have I

that I can find

someone like you

before I die.

Everything I am or do,

will be of you

as I struggle through life

until the day that I am able

just to say,

Thank you, for walking in my mind,

alongside me

along our way.

But, today for you?

I am unworthy.

Ti's not your loss

but is all mine,

your shining bright,

your light,

just for me to see.

More will come

but for you and for me

our time will come.

The hope of this will

let us see

that the ones who love

you or me,

will be the one meant to be!

I am just unworthy!

Blessed am I for you,

if I walk true,

and do not lie,

someday one like you

will walk by my side.

Better yet would be if I,

could walk along side

one as you,

and then my happiness

would be really true!

To be of a simple birth

to shine in your eyes,

willing to love and live,

and in your eyes

have worth,

But not today.

It takes all I have

to exist,

alone and unwanted.

No matter how my soul cries-

you are a ray of hope

the steepness of the hill I travel

is of lesser slope.

You need better than me,

some day after you have

forgotten one as me,

In your life,

I will never cross again -

and I will fade away,

the same way,

day after day,

until you have what you deserve:

One not of damage,

but one who loves

the way your belly curves;

True wonder. To never give you

a thought to ponder -

just giggling with

the itty bitty you both hold

in wonder!

Not even a memory,

or a sense of wonder,

will you think of me

as I go yonder.

finding Forester

Sent: Thu 11/05/09 10:12 PM

Sometimes, the only thing to do is to start typing

and when you feel your words, let them loose!

I am sick and you need to do what you have to do,

but I can have another pinner!

And after burnt, I will think of you

and what we should be able to have,

Of course this doesn't rhyme and

I don't give a fuck!

You had your chance and of course,

your path was chosen,

But not your course!

I do not want any rebuke,

but soon I hear from you,

or else,

I just puke!

You hold my soul dearly,

and in it I trust,

the truth I need to hear,

or my dick will turn to dust!

I cannot wait for you to send

a note to me

to break my heart.

I want! Gimme that! I don't care!

I get it now,

or you will pay!

I'll steal it when you're are away!

So pay me now, or pay when

the cost will go unnoticed.

If you can't ask, and you can't be

Honest just a tad,

I should put a bullet in your brain and then play modest!

But the real truth is

you need to be dead

and I am way to honest!

RE: finding forrester

Sent: Thu 11/05/09 11:20 PM

Too often we do fail, as we cry,

unable to tell what makes us sigh.

The truth comes out to those we love,

who do nothing but let us!

In return, never ask for what is not given,

the sin is not of us but only those well striven!

The price we pay is not ours and then we walk away,

but each of us will pay the price and never know what to say.

The pain of what they did do,

their hearts were truly pure,

but harm and scars are what is left,

we have none to do with this;

The minutes turn to decades,

instead of just of hours!

Hold dear the pain that lingers in your heart,

as this is only yours!

The bullshit they put us through,

will let us open doors.

It may seem that they inflict the harm

that we may feel

but we can always walk away,

and fuck up their deal!

I thought I asked for help,

but that was not the case.

How was I to know that they

played with the cased Ace?

"Not fair!" You say, yet where is that

written?

Just lick your nuts

do not be smitten, as

your heart is pure, and

it is not hidden.

Relax and breath, as it should be,

survive this now and you will see,

that what they did,

will cost dearly,

and you walk away freely!

No pain, no gain,

and all this bullshit,

it only becomes ours

when we accept it!

If you don't

Then need not be said,

a failure he was not, yet

even if it came to be,

"fuck you!!" You did not help

in hours of need!

the storm of shit!

Sent: Fri 11/06/09 12:35 PM

Why is it that those of us who connect

are always a dire threat?

No harm was sent,

and no one wanted for us to get,

but even still

a storm of shit

splatters our soul-

with a deadly hit!

A chink in our armor

shows the way,

for pain to come

by what they say.

We took the chance to

touch a soul

from deep within our hearts

the result will always be

just like a wet fart!

No one else will know,

that where we walk,

or where we go,

will touch as we talk,

yet it hurts us to the bone.

Now for me I fill my

Peterson,

Mac Baren Burly Flake

to sooth my soul,

instead of my gun.

I should not smoke this,

I know,

but a

match well-lit will also show,

that deeply hidden

in my soul,

an old man's self-indulgence

of an old man's tobacco

opens up my own grave

and keeps me from being a winner.

So, fuck it all! I am not brave!

Next I will smoke a pinner:

the appetite that comes

will surely enhance

the taste

of my own dinner!

I hope your day went smooth

and was not too bitter,

my bottle is empty,

so here comes that pinner!

No matter what they do

or what they say,

when your time comes,

I've lit the way!

Never warp from your

own way.

No blow, nor strike

should sway you from your path.

I should feel guilty for the shit I send-Read this first!!

Sent: Fri 11/06/09 5:46 PM

I hope your evening was spent in heart felt joy,

not as a tool or weapon,

but as a toy;

something that gives us pleasure,

without thinking of what we spent

to gain the treasure!

"Save yourself, kill them all!"

from Hannibal the cannibal!

The word of others has its value,

to touch our soul,

and guide us well

down our avenue!

A bumpy row to hoe,

with all its clods,

to touch my heart and

never hear,

the sounds of my own sobs.

Tonight was fun, your work is done,

and now is time to rest,

disregard all my shit,

but use it well,

for your best!

Call when you can.

I love you t,

Grandpa al, an old man.

'tis only 11:48 and not a word from you

Sent: Sat 11/07/09 12:05 AM

I do not handle rejection well, so what more can I say?

I've shown you how bent I am,

 the price I will pay!

But so it is as it is and, nothing more to say.

Your dragons fly against the wind,

I'm always standing at your back;

loaded gun and steadfast

always one you can count on,

but when you look at your rear,

will be me standing there,

live your life and never fear!

My whole purpose in life

was to be where you needed me,

and not a word of harsh was spoken,

the scars I bear are only mine,

a mere token!

For if not for mine,

and you for me,

what sense is there in dressing?

now you have me pissed!

Sent: Sun 11/08/09 2:00 PM

I know that you screen your calls and that is how it should be

but all I want is just to say, "Go to your computer, and when you

have a chance, read and then call me!"

I wanted to send you two of mine,

one to make you cry and

the other to make you shit

but your mail box is full,

I might as well have went outside

and shouted at the moon,

so dull!

Tis only for you I write this wonder

not for you, but for me,

and now you have me pissed off.

It could come to pass

that words no longer

come your way

and even if I don't like that,

this you must own:

you have a say

in some of that!!

Clean your fucking mail box out!!!!

You have your dick to get wet,

the ground awaits for me!

Am I being selfish as an old man?

Or, do you want to hear this shit,

before I die?

Could it be that you want a full fucking

mail box to decide,

the protection of who you

talk to, and the reasons why?

You missed out

on a really neat

thingy

you break my nuts instead of talking to me

so, no more to you I

bringy!!

RE: what it was really like, and why I don't want to talk about it

Sent: Sun 11/08/09 2:00 PM

Hi t, I know that you have things to do, and I sit here with nothing to do,

so I will write some shit from my soul and send to you!

Only when you have this kind of shit, hit and hurt,

with a direct hit, the question arises:

Will you tell? Or relive all of the different hells,

that they did without a thought

of the tolling bell?

Will they see me with all of my charms or,

only see my father's harms?

The answer lies in the ground -

Long, dead and cold!

No Mother for me to learn from,

and no one to love and hold,

and relish in her sound.

We stood there in our Sunday best,

and it was said, "They know not

what we know, and that is the best.

Look at the little darlings!

They stand there without knowing

their Mother we lay to Rest!"

We had been told that morning,

gray and cold,

"No blubbering and no bawling!

I am not having you'sss

embarrass me, or hell

you's will surely pay!"

So we stood there,

two small girls clinging to my legs

and we knew.

The stare from a rattle snake,

had nothing on her look.

Into the ground our lives

were thrust.

Damage done and the price to pay,

we carried all for us, even to this day.

We were young and we were there,

but the venom that dripped

from her stare,

kind of killed the love for Grandmother

that cold and painful day!

Her heart of rock and stone,

she carried like a badge

and none of them carried

the weight of what we ferried,

But still faced, there we stood;

our mother into the ground,

and more than any other

we truly understood!

the very last if you don't empty your fucking mailbox!

Sent: Sun 11/08/09 3:46 PM

Sunday morning early came bright

a clear full starry night

four hours before first light

with chores to do, I must

not lose sight!

The hens to water, gather eggs,

the butcher calves well fed,

four buckets for milk did I carry,

empty bellied, I must not tarry.

The only joy of this day was the

comfort of the clean cow smell,

with hay!

I lay my head against her flank,

breathed in, and enjoyed

the way I felt.

The milk bucket held firmly by my knees,

my hands hurt lightly as I squeezed,

the milk flowed soft with a foam,

and she ate deeply of the extra grain,

just her and me, all alone.

The knots built up on slow earned pain,

and still bulge out, to this day.

Never did she kick or complain

as the bucket filled,

my wrists complained.

Now the other was a different story,

a red brindled bitch,

born as ornery as a snake,

a kick let loose,

my own my mistake!

My boots were covered in that milk

that flew across the floor,

nothing meaner did I see

except when I stepped

through Grandma's door!

Their hearts were made of

things gone bad,

it was not their fault,

but still they took their joy!

A swift kick here, a wordy blow there,

and who was the target?

I let them out to the pasture

and to the house I lived,

to the separator..

now hungry, I need to get

ready for Mass.

The light was here for a while

my belly did make it's grumble

into Church I did walk

even If I stumbled.

The air was dead,

the heat was hot,

when my turn came

to partake

of her good Lord's

soul to taste.

And so it came to be

that all this

was a prelude

for when my turn was there.

I raised my mouth

so I could taste

the salvation there,

but the light went out,

and back I fell,

into the pew I hit.

I came too outside the Church,

my head was truly split!

Carried by four men of

strong, they took me to her

car,

and on the ride home

I came to bear the displeasure

in the air!

"How could you embarrass me

with all your disgrace,

when father smiled on your face?!

For all I've done to raise you right,

you throw this in my face!

It is all you do, every time!

You'ss are my disgrace!" She did holler.

In the backseat of the Pontiac,

my tears did flow.

Of course I passed out,

all my choice,

it was all I wanted,

to pass out in the church!

Her center of the universe,

must have been lonely,

there was no room for

a child, she filled it up only!

That withered old bitch, had the chance

to sooth my soul,

but what she wanted

was me dead

and into my own Hole!

The night before

at supper time,
I took a verbal beating,

of all the food on the table,

no joy could I take eating.

To all of them, I was an

animal, not worth the

trouble of being wild,

just another mouth to feed!

No thanks could I give

to such a rich table,

they did not give,

of free will; of what

they were not able!

The supper Grace had

been given,

this would only hurt:

I took their blows, and I

swallowed, knowing I must

shirk all their barbs and all their hate.

<u>okay think about this now</u>

Sent: Sun 11/08/09 5:57 PM

If I dog your calls, for a month or two,

and you want to see me,

it could be that time will tell

the grass grows on my

spot of ground.

Or, I may not be found!

and so it will be!

Re: beautiful

Sent: Sun 11/08/09 9:26 PM

Great job!

We do choose and stand our ground,

the fault is theirs and not our sound

but fuck, just fuck 'em!

p.s. I like your lines

as you should know

and only, can I nudge

to gently push you

on your path.

I don't understand the shit

that people do,

but the scars of what they've

done, casts a shadow on my

babies.

The fault of that,

on my shoulders,

and only cause

too dumb was I

to see the spuds

and gravies!

We do the shit we do

we have no other options

too stupid we seem to be,

to see what can stops us!

The harm we did and the

harm we do, should not

land on a child,

we think the world has shit

on us,

but not on a child!

It was our responsibility to

ensure,

that the children we left,

did not endure!

The fault was never theirs to bare

but only those who are dead.

With damage done,

and scars to feel,

we do not pay the price

but to them, it is what we left.

Sad tears,

to them comes a monster,

and today they must deal

with shit we cannot muster.

The harm we did for our own greed,

we left the cost of that to feed

upon our youngest!

"Fuck 'em" is what we say,

it is only what I wanted!

It is not my fault

that one of them who

marches on unwanted

will tell the tale of those of us that

did what we could do,

just to get us what we wanted!

So, fucked we were,

and fucked we are - and,

you can kiss my ass!

The worst that can happen upon

my grave, is growing green grass!

<u>my best of times</u>

Sent: Thu 11/12/09 11:33 PM

The best of times for me

were when Mass was done and

In the middle of the dry-belt of central Wyoming,

Grandpa owned the only irrigated land

and was the only one

without his soul

owed to a bank.

And he'd smile,

for all he had done

and all he had left

paid his way - the last hard mile

none of his he thought

would ever need his smile

and of course, the weakest ones

were those to sit at his meager table

the eldest son saw all this as a threat

and enemy defined.

Too bad they were unable

to have the clout to pay the

price of those

who lived so fine.

But when they live the Bible ,

they will see

that I own them all

and all they dream

fore I am the eldest -

Piss not upon my grave

for what I did,

I really did!

And, not for the children,

but, as it states,

In the book,

the oldest gets all this fucking shit!

So when that fucker died

none of us who had

a voice would shed a tear

or cry!

Of course it is our fault

that fuck-head went into

the ground,

without a candle lit..

but, what the fuck?

You never had to

step into the steps

of my sister dear!

Her steps alone

as she walked

would try the soul

you hold dear!

I think the path

that I walked

never had.

heres one that will sunday punch the skinny bitch! you're gonna
love this

Sent: Mon 11/30/09 2:53 AM

I hobbled up to your grave site

heart heavy and full of tears

what you missed out

of only 27 years

without the sound of

the little bitties,

who carry your spirit

and your sounds of joy.

Fifty some years have passed

and still

the look of the hole

in the ground they put you

with my face slapped red

from your mother..

she missed all that you gave

of what to enjoy

and when to be brave.

Your heart I carry on as if

it was my own

but the itty bitties

all love you,

even if they don't know!

I kneel on the hard cold gumbo

where I could not shed a tear

as I needed to that day,

who claimed to be your mother,

dropped a Benjamin into

the sin plate!

No slobbering

or any of that bawling,

"you will not disgrace me"

and that is as the blow,

came to my face.

I stood there, solid, firm,

with my tiny sisters hanging

on to me,

as if I knew what to do.

You who loved us, gone

what will I do?

Who will sing your song?

We stood there as strangers

inspected us and said the

things that remain today,

"Those poor babies don't

even know what is happening!"

Well, we stood there as our mother

deep into the ground went,

no one to help us, only

the ones who want us well

beaten, and well bent!

But it was not your fault

that the darkness came

before us,

and took you away,

the money went into

the sin plate while the Priest

said all was good with God,

and it was His will..

"Support the Church, and God

will ease your pain, take care

of the children."

The cactus wants to stick me

but that was done years ago

we outlived all of yours, and

we came out well bent!

Failures. All of us. Well, those

that still live

but your soul has

given us all we needed

to teach us to give!

Oh, we look hard to find that

but it is there under the dirt

just like you, and we should not shirk.

You did not have the chance to see

and love those of the ones we gave life to

no one to know that it was you who

touched with love upon on your small ones.

We don't know why we take care of the

small ones, but they think we walk on water.

Long ago, we laid you to rest

and even if you never know,

all of us tried our very best.

None of us have tried to shirk

of what you gave,

but we watched you

into your grave.

Knee high, young and soft

we stood there while your family

planted you,

knowing only that we could not morn

and let them see us shed a tear,

at your going.

What we did not see, or

while we were growing,

was your touch in our hearts

and in our souls!

We paid the price for you leaving soon,

ridiculed, abused, and well used.

We had no defense for your departing

but our tickets were well punched!

No chance to get a better deal

or even barter!

I was pissed at you for being dead

and then my time came,

nothing I can do to ensure that

the itty bitties don't go through the

hell that all of us went through,

but they all will mourn when

GG and me are gone, and

if we are lucky,

one or more will have

a soft thought, or even sing a

song.

How do I come to grips with you gone

so soon,

my being fucked up as a loon

and yet, the babies love my

touch? Where did that come from?

Except, you did what you could do.

A hard line in the ground drawn by you.

No quarter given, except to the little

ones, my time is at hand

and I leave nothing so grand.

I tried, failed , and sometimes

I wonder if all those I leave

will have thoughts of me,

or will they wish that

I had just dug in

and made my stand?

Even if they never know,

all I did, all I wanted

was for them to have a soft

thought, whenever I have to go.

On the stone above me

just carve,

"I did good and I failed miserably!"

The Devil's ass was kissed

long before I had a chance!

and then fuck it all,

I will do my own dance!

<u>when do I get more??? like ,, never!!</u>

Sent: Fri 12/11/09 8:17 PM

Oh, too bad, too sad,

slam your dick in the door!

I refuse to give you good stuff

and all you do is ignore!

So from now on,

my mail box is full,

don't send mail, and don't

call!

My heart is broken and

can't be fixed,

I'm smoking weed and

drinking rum,

I bet my nuts,

you wish you had

some!!

Too little, too late,

with nothing to say,

so- I am fucked up

but just for today!

Oh! And fuck you,

fuck you!

Fw: Re:

Sent: Mon 12/28/09 8:39 PM

When I looked into the glass

to brush my teeth

and scratch my ass,

yet to me, I hid my smile,

my path laid out,

a crooked mile.

So when I looked to see,

I saw a coward

staring back at me.

Re: aw shit

Sent: Sat 1/23/10 4:17 PM

I was being shaken!

"This cannot be good!" I thought in that split second between my rapid eye movement sleep, with your eye balls rocking and a-rolling and when your body is at full rest and it feels so good. I went from that to Damn! Shit! Piss! Fuck! "This cannot be good!" I thought.

In the last four years, I have learned that if you are awaken in the morning, before anyone else, this day is going to be like when the Pilgrim climbed up to the Dali Llama and asked, "Can you give me the meaning of life!?"

The Dali Llama replied, "Well, when you stick your finger in a tiger's ass, all the way up to the last knuckle, from that point on, not much good is going to happen that day!"

That is what it was like to be shaken awake! No matter what, nothing good was going to happen that day! It was the House Fairy, well, that's what I called that mule dicked, monkey meat, power, abuser and pedophile that I was forced to live with.

His official title was House Father!

I am ten years old. And my worst trait is that I know how to survive, without coming into the spotlight! I know that if I do that, it is only me that will pay that terrible price, just like the kid named Gary, who I liked, and he liked me. Neither one of us was a threat to each other. That really speaks to the shit we had to live with, and the rules that allowed me to find someone who cared about me as much as I cared about him!

And Poof! he was gone. It seems that his father came home early, and found Gary with fourteen inches of really hard cock, shoved rapidly as fast as he could, into his stepmother! The obituary said that it was a crime of passion, and it was so sad, that one bullet claimed two lives.

Poof! Gone!

No one in my corner to patch up my fuckups! Just me! At ten. I knew not to make fuckups!

shit house philosophers

Sent: Sun 5/09/10 10:12 PM

At nine years old, I took a step,

down my path of no regrets.

On my own, no one cared,

or offered a shoulder to share.

I walked alone, unafraid,

into the shit others made.

Defenseless and on my own,

where the fuck did I go?

This bucket of shit

was mine to carry.

Forty nine years after I

was I married,

the terms of what I said

to myself,

became muddied,

witha small price to be paid!

For I promised only for my

lifetime, not hers!

Not a lifetime of being harried!

Selfish, self-serving, what more can I say?

In this marriage,

I try to be everything

what was not there for me.

None of those whom paid for Heaven,

knew it was me who counted their dollars

for the Priest!

Small and defenseless,

What chance did I have or

what could they sell??

I walked on, down my path,

who could have known,

I really had God's wrath!

A child young and little,

is an easy target with a heart,

not yet old enough to be brittle.

The hardness came with experience,

all the child needs to see,

that what happens to the

little ones,

no power, no hope, no chance to help,

and that is what the child

carried down his path as his own failure!

Now my Grandmother, my mother's mother,

hated me as if I was a sin.

The Priest used this to extort

a horrible bulk of money

without penitence.

Within an hour of being without a mother,

my father told me to make ready, my

little brother and my sisters!

"Now they all are your responsibility."

 and he drove off

 not be seen for a decade, or so.

So if you want to throw a wet and sloppy wad of

shit, one I will not dodge,

have a go!

She had two score and a half,

to back-stab, and sabotage,

for the gifts she gave.

Today, I realize,

I received Gifts from God

And and Linda and get old

all my children are safe and

healthy! Not selfish, with hearts of gold.

When I have to take my place

into the hole,

I go knowing

where is safe!

Doing one's best, often

leaves, a very bitter taste.

still no email from you
Sent: Sat 5/15/10 10:22 PM

I am ending, you are beginning,

and still I have a gift to give,

the pain of living all my years,

should smoothen your path,

and let you live.

Make your music to these lyrics, and see

what you get.

Play what you have written, and play it

while you pick a lead guitar to the above lyrics!

Believe me, you music is way beyond great,

but it is not finished! Think on it after you

get done being pissed at me!!

My words were never meant to harm,

but only add to your special charm! -gpa al

so-- we are back to this kind of shit??!!
Sent: Tue 6/15/10 11:50 AM

Again I want to talk to you,

but your fucking phone is full,

I had good shit to tell you,

but your fucking phone is full!

Broken hearted here I sit,

while I feel rejected.

When I cannot communicate with you,

after all that I have tried,

you pissed me off enough,

to cut your nuts and fry!

Instead I stare at the blank email,

and never feel respected.

This morning my heart has crumbled to dust

eagerly I go to email to hear music sent,

but once again I am left down on my knees,

they would not stay straight, now fully bent!

A small tantrum I did have,

my phone was in flight,

it's guts are scattered on the floor

the wall put up a fight.

The ache of not getting instant gratification

when I hear your lyrics and notes,

is like when I pissed in the lake

over the side of my boat!

..A small line of bubbles, and the fish puked,

and now you stand, fully rebuked!

hey?! Hey?! this fucking one is gonna cost you! it is good

Sent: Sun 6/20/10 4:59 PM

Yea, you are easy to corrupt,

with just one true thought,

your nuts are bruised,

in the zipper caught!

Screaming won't help, and no one's touch,

will knock the teeth off the zipper,

cause you will have a better time

trying to find a virgin stripper!

Bob does not count!

the ugly fuck!

delivered not by the stork,

but by a duck!

Bring him home, and go to sleep,

and never have a thought about him,

as we weep,

the road of life is often long,

and now Goddamn it, it's raining!

With wet gumbo at the Church,

collection plates still strong,

without knowing,

their path has grown.

Straight up, wet, coming down,

and only in a family loved,

will what we reap, is what we have sown!

<u>you gotta tell me what you think</u>
Sent: Wed 9/01/10 2:12 PM

Hi, I am guessing that by now you know that my sister died this morning at about 12;30 AM.

Here is some shit I wrote, let me really know what you think.

With a heavy heart, broken, bruised, shredded,

the pain will not sink in until I touch your forehead.

No warmth, just cold, to my touch,

even if you are not old.

But the itty bitties that you leave in

your wake,

looked at you and your warrior heart,

scared deep and slowly roasted in hell,

not done for yours, but their own sake.

But they all will cry tonight when you

do not show up, just to let them know

that the morning will bring a sound,

a soft bell.

The trueness of your soul shows in all of us,

who feel with a heavy heart forever,

that still feels as if ,

our hearts took a turn through a meat grinder.

The world is flatter today without you being here.

What should we all do?

How do we march into the unknown without

your grace to guide us?

You left us when we needed you the most.

Sit at God's table and show us how to be the host.

The tracks you left on all of our hearts run deep,

and it runs true, even now when you sleep.

Cold and not forgotten, you live on in all our

hearts and memories,

not something that drifts into the deep.

You were loved and all of that sits on your shoulders,

worn wide and strong from your life's path.

Never dodging or whining your way clear,

but into the storm you marched,

heart wide open,

and even with fear,

you strode into life, dealt a shitty hand of cards,

you lived your life -

We all hold all of you dear!

Orphaned at eight and abandoned in the same hour,

I showed us how to eat by stealing just a little.

Take a slice of bread,

we steal a slab of baloney,

not all! Just enough for our bellies to feel full.

And we will see if tomorrow we eat at

Maloney's!

Back we come to Safeway, but not

for a week or two..

we were hungry, not stupid.

It could be said that you were a

battle hardened survivor,

but the small little girl stills

resides, inside your soft soul.

But, "Fuck 'em" is what you said, and what you

Showed;

The strength of a Mother, Grandmother, and

most of all, a Sister, and a friend,

you carried on your arm and sleeve,

for all to look at and still see!

You did your job well.

None of those whom

you've touched in your life,

will come close to the shit from your past

as if it were not there.

Sleep well, Sister loved,

rest at ease, you did your job

same as a ring necked dove,

That sighs in the time

Just before dark.

Loved and precious were you before you

became unavailable—

but rest assured, you are loved and missed

by us all!

I wish I could have stood up to the same standard

you lived your life by.

And if they missed understanding,

they could go fuck themselves;

they were not worthy!

Sleep well Sissy,

I join in a moment soon.

<u>bull shit and other stuff</u>
Sent: Sun 4/24/11 5:58 PM

The secret kept, the truth comes out

and makes us lower flags to half-mast

so instead of my asshole slamming shut

so I could choke a railroad spike in half

I turned the monster loose, and out in the light

a solution found, no war to fight!

With a silver tongue, well-greased words

comes out of the south end of a north bound bird

no matter how I want this to pass

it is my sound and my goat smelling ass.

I stand here before you, naked and unafraid

with no tools or weapons, as it was forbade

take your shot and aim well as

nothing hurts while I live in Hell.

Your wants and needs come dearly to me

I owe you that and hope you see!

Not a threat but a real small child

no one to help, no one to guide

the best to be done is to run

and hide- but not so easy.

The owl cries, it is a rigged game

you cannot win.

So carry your scars well hidden,

bound up in pain, and still forbidden

no one can know, no one can care,

no one looks at you with

a heartfelt stare,

the trouble came and then it went,

and next to that , I was sent!

Away!

 (No Subject)

Sent: Wed 4/27/11 5:26 AM

to come out from under warn quilts,

secure, comfort!

Breakfast in the morning,

lunch at noon.

a sound ass beating

when school got out!

No idea of why,

or who was to blame!

What the fuck did I do?

A hard pill to swallow,

one that chokes!

Too bad you were not

up to task, maybe you

need more coke?

<u>unexpected words of prose</u>

Sent: Sun 5/01/11 8:09 PM

We all use words in their special order of line

some are easy to read, some are hard to find.

Some tell of hard emotions, some are sold

as angel's lotion!

But the truth of the words we write,

are but grist for our souls to grind.

We each touch the souls of the ones we love,

the rest are roasted, toasted, and enjoyed

like a slow cooked dove!

Yet to all of us who share our soul's thought,

touch the true value that cannot be bought.

Families that only war,

miss out on the strength,

to just take one more fucking

step and find the glory!

Only families who share

secrets, feel their pain,

and have the strength to

grow though all of it!

To be strong, is to be weak

for if that is what you want,

the winning ways will be

short, the winners

will think of themselves

as anything but

to kiss a duck's ass

without touching a

feather!

Whew! Smack--

is all it takes,

are you weak

or strong enough?

That truth only comes

out of your great

grandchildren!

If you are strong enough-

to take one more fucking step!

so good to talk to you
Sent: Wed 5/04/11 9:09 PM

No one has the value

of time spent until

you are an old man.

What do you do when

the hours turn the day into

forever?

And all it will take for the

day to be right,

is a line or two from you,

and my day is bright!

After the sand in the glass

has fallen,

when time is long past short

that we finally see what

we have done,

and who we did it with

tells if we were wrong,

or we went through the

wringer, with the right

one!

When the scars of this

show on our bodies,

we all come together

and we tell our lies!

Time is shorter than

you think,

soon worms will devour

my flesh,

and gone I will be.

The return may save our

Soul, and keep the dragons

from our homes.

But when all turns dark,

only those of stout heart,

will step forward and pay-

so all of us, sleep well,

today.

bullshit and other ramblings

Sent: Mon 5/09/11 6:29 PM

The clock goes off at an early hour,

I am still tired as I dress for the day.

I could have planned for this, and I did,

first is to milk the cows, feed the

butcher hogs, and their winter beef.

No matter what, don't spill the milk!

Run the separator, save the cream.

Wash the milk pails, go up stairs

and choke down great food as I

again hear grandma's tirade and

screams.

The eggs are the best that eggs

can be, fresh from the farm,

as I know, I take care of them, and

now I want to eat,

but the harsh words do insure

that I do not forget,

that all I am

is a mistake,

and curdle my food.

I only sat at their table

because of their great

need to look good

to their neighbors and

we never ate rice!

I was beget

my cloths all folded in a pile,

school attire on right, and

I am on my way

to the only peace for

me to only three miles that way.

Sanctuary!

The first two weeks of school

with all of my books well read,

to ace all weekly and quarterly tests.

Back home, all they gave was righteous,.

they did God's work,

and the wheat would grow!

Their wealth and grace

came from the skies,

God insured they knew that

they all were graced,

and the ones unworthy

paid their price!

Dead, lost, and disgraced,

they left their brats to

look at each new day

and saddled hem with making the children pay,

for what they did not know.

The Midst of Chaos
Sent: Thu 5/12/11 10:13 PM

I lived with the wealthiest people in the county. And in the
town, no matter what, they owned the second and the third
Pew in Church, no matter what!
The grandfather clock towered over me, and its ten o'clock bell
filled the silence throughout the hall, leaving an echo as its last
strike passed. I rubbed my eye, staring at the reflection of the
lamp in the glass. There was always an unbearably painful stick
jabbed deep in my chest wherever I walked, slept, sat or stood
in that mansion of phony power and royalty. Having not entered
this: 'my family'- until the age of ten, and looking the complete
opposite of anybody else around, I was the outcast. Constantly
questioned and corrected for every single step I took, whether it
was small or gigantic. In their eyes I was always majorly
displeasing and at very least, a letdown. I fell asleep there, on
that thick brown carpet dreaming of a black airplane.

As I finally fully awoke the next morning, I was told again to
the choke down one fried egg, my now cold slice of toast and
the other half of my orange. I was prompt to inhale the fried
egg and cold slice of toast, but slammed nose first into a cement
wall when I realized all I had left was the orange. A fucking
orange! Oh Lord! It was a set-up, just another opportunity to be
ground into the crust of the dirt and shredded to dust powder.
You see, they all could take a tea spoon, stick it between the

rind and the peel, and use it like a mystic. The chunk of fruit would jump out of the peel like a cat that had just slipped and sunk his ass in a boiling pot of pig fat, and they all looked at me like I was the Antichrist! Of course they have been doing this since birth, come on, they were rich and privileged- while I was not.

They all glanced at each other shaking their heads; at this table surrounded by royalties and then me, as I gnawed at that half an orange like a dog on a fresh deer kill. I wiped the juice off my chin before it could drip and ruin the one of a kind tablecloth that my grandmother held so sacred. I got up and set my plate in the sink, and pushed in my chair . I noticed my pencil in the dining room floor and still to this day I do not understand how the fuck it ended up there.

The anticipation grew more and more unbearable as the time grew closer to seven. The wind screamed across the tree tops and just as I looked out the window of the study, shoved a trash can down on the sidewalk. "You better get your ass walking if you're planning on making to school on time!" my grandmother bellowed from the other room. I smiled. Finally, freedom was attainable.

As a child of confusion, irreparable damage from abandonment, and a lack of defenses, this long walk to school was my sanctuary despite the unrelenting wind which ripped the hood of my jacket that I paid for 'out of my inheritance' off my head the second I opened the door.

I stepped into the bitter cold west wind straight into the face of a fierce winter blizzard. Biting shards of frozen moisture hit my face with the veracity of a pissed off Grizzly bear who's cubs are in danger. That didn't matter. I had a whopping three and a half mile to walk to school which served as a big safe cushion for me to enjoy. As I walked steadily with hands deep in pockets, everything inside my skin sunk. Thinking about breakfast at grandma's table developed into bigger wads of familiar bowling ball feelings with each step. And to think I was just getting over the sting of being told again of my true worth to anyone or anything the previous Monday. For me, that was the normal conversation that floated my way at every meal. They always told me the same thing and they always had the same effect on me. They always meant every single cruel work, and with that I became small but protected inside.

The raw arctic air assaulted me as I held my chin up with my shoulders back and walked through my sanctuary. For the next three miles, until school, I was free and safe. Nothing now could sting, bite and slice me with the precision of a samurai swinging a sword, like their words. Though, this alone time was my emotional safe haven, I was psychically as vulnerable as a freshly hatched robin under a starving eagle. That didn't matter. This walk was the highlight, the limelight time of every day after every dreaded sunrise and absolutely nothing was going to screw it up for me. No matter what, it was all up to me to walk through my time of peace which still to this day is absolutely precious to me.

I entered the school house and immediately a wave of safety and heat plowed over my body. My eyes closed half way and glossed over in this moment of orgasm, to enter worry free environment which was so distant and unrealistic to me. As usual, I smiled and school seemed surreal to me but was soon to be kicked down, reviving my frown. I moved towards the classroom

I was the kind of student who made the teachers and counselors say to themselves and their peers, 'there is something about that boy that makes me sure that I chose the right profession." They seen me as a twisted and far too disengaged rat in the back that didn't have a chance. This troubled me, and eventually I gave up resisting their attempts at chipping through to me because I truly understood how important my education was and I wanted to prove that to them all! I was always denied opportunity, and when it proved itself evident, I didn't hesitate to take advantage of it. So these teachers assigned bull crap that they actually believed. I studied hard and aced all of their tests. Not to impress them, but to let me know that their educational effort; their contribution to society, was not wasted on me. In doing do, I showed each and every one of them what was, and still is, inside of me, which they could not deal with. I was always just quiet enough to leave all of them shaking their heads and wondering to themselves just how to shape me into being something they could take credit for, but no one dared to try to break me simply because I lived with the wealthiest people in the county. And in the town, no matter what, they owned the second and the third Pew in Church! No matter what! I tallied the collection plate after Mass, every Sunday. It took a while, but I soon realized that each one of those filthy pig bible thumpers put a hundred dollar check in the plate every week, yet I paid for my board and room out of my personal 'inheritance'. They gave nothing freely, and that is to be the unspoken conclusion of all I write.

(No Subject)
Sent: Sun 5/22/11 7:21 PM

So here I sit alone,

my choice, my own

to suffer while my

family disintegrates.

The third divorce and

felony fired gun

puts my grandchild

in harm's way,

let alone what her mother

went through!

But still I am not

allowed to say

that logic, reason

and experience

will show another way!

As trailer load after

load goes into

mine and my wife's

landlord's basement,

such a small price to pay.

I do love her and her sisters,

I won't forget to remind them today.

Rejection is a constant

companion,

that we are not good at

seeing what we should do!

But in the piles of rubble

lay busted hearts,

wasted dreams

and a determination

to do the same fucking

thing tomorrow!

I fertilize the pain,

as I lie,

to a small great

grandchild

when I told her

she could fly.

No wonder she fell!

The best I can do

is try to undo, the harm.

One lesson learned,

keep clear of bullshit.

We all wade through

the pain of choices

 that all have made,

and when the family

draws together,

to support the one in shit,

the foundation is made!

Take a breath, take a step,

see how well you have done.

And at the end of the race,

we'll see who has lost,

and who has won?!

what do you think?
Sent: Tue 5/24/11 6:05 PM

A dark and dreary wet kind of day,

Insulted from a child we raised

hard overcast, steady rain- a soaker

rain, needed for a crop, farmers prayed.

In the backyard, under the lilacs, and

under the tree of plum,

lay sleeping a pair of mature

mule deer bucks.

I stop and ask why I am blessed to see,

what no one else in the middle of our

Cultural Center, in the center of our city,

can see -

and there they lay.

The trout feed heavily on a day like this,

and food comes to them in the wet,

my ass is soaked, my clothes will take

time to dry.

The creel is heavy as I trudge to

the parking lot at the end of

a gravel road,

the deer rest easy in the back yard,

and inside my skin, solitude lays light,

no injuries, nothing done wrong, and

the deer do not take flight!

Fried creek trout, fun, and fried

to a crisp,

give peace to all, who sit at

my table tonight.

The bounty of this good earth,

comes to those who earn it—

which makes me wonder why

this gift was freely given to mine;

how do I deserve it?

If we live the best we can live,

and we hold true to the knowledge,

that all we have to do is help all of ours..

Not our job to judge, but just to be there,

and all tickets for admission are well paid.

When we are comfortable in our skins,

Seeking solitude and ease,

we watch the mule deer in the back yard,

who have the same thing we have.

And they know, chewing today's cud,

with ease of being, in the calm of a lilac

bush,

If it gets bad, we can run!

I pray to be able to chew

my cud in my own back yard,

but will never be

I am too damaged, and the harm done

will spill over to the soft life given when

the sky leaks,

the Mule deer knows,

the farmer grows,

the ignorant plants rows,

what we harvest

we will re-sow!

Just like the Mule deer, I

Seek solitude when all

I need do for the day

Is chew my cud!

If I am gifted with

you, then all I have done,

was done so I

support you.

Will you do the same stupid shit

that was done?

Will the chain be broken,

are you the one

who makes a home

you can keep?

The truth comes out

on a rainy day,

I tell my soul

that all I want is

for the all of us to be good.

The gentle rest under bushes,

no gun, no threat, no nightmares,

rest easy, rest soft, take your time

for when you wake,

again you face

the same shit

all of mine face

just the same,

as all of you face.

<u>here is a small token, it took a while to do this,so</u>
Sent: Tue 6/07/11 3:11 AM

On the way to school,

after a long morning in the dark

chores to do, separate the milk,

harsh words with eggs and

farm fresh bread toast.

My morning started at 4:00 AM.

Out of bed, not to be a disappointment.

To the crow, her name hid deep in the

secret bottom of my soul!

The fresh smell of the milk cows,

eagerly welcomed, just for that touch

of comfort, and a soft reassurance

came through my nose, as I pulled up

my stool, rested my forehead in her

flank, to feel when she kicked!

With a mouth full of grain,

contentment ran all the way to

the switch that lets milk down.

But when I push open the main door

to the barn, I am caressed with the smell of

hay and horses-, contentment caresses

all of me!

The soft fragrance of a living

barn

soaks into my soul,

lets me know that all

is right in my world.

The ground is flat again,

without my control!

I know nothing here will hurt me,

as there is no harm when I feed

and stroke the stock, not a kick

or a switch of a tail- different

from the breakfast table

where I will take my hits,

when I should be able

to eat without being a fable.

The oatmeal turns lumpy

when fed with insults from

those around the table.

I did my chores, did them well,

even cleaned the stable!

Inside my skin, at eleven,

I had no fault with me,

but my ticket into hell

was free, and

all I had to be, was there..

Not a hard sell.

Uncles let me know

how much I was wanted

and how much it pleased

them to keep me in hell

but only if I let them know

that their words cut like

a samurai sword.

Head up high, I looked

back as if I did not understand

too dumb to know better,

but I got to stay there

as long as I worked hard-

A free farmhand.

I was the real problem,

too young to

pay for board

not worth the food

they gave me as they

told me how much I

was paying to be there.

Family secrets kept

even from the Priest

did not scare me like

being discarded again.

Where would the next stop be?

What do I do to be ok here?

Everything I own fits in

a paper bag from

the grocery store.

Not a big bag, just

holds two pair of socks,

one extra shirt-

last month's shorts,

but not a place to live

or be welcome.

But I take to the

grave without being

forced to confess!

It was my fault-

too young to know better,

too weak to fulfill the role of whipping boy!

<u>so here is another one about you and me.</u>
Sent: Sun 6/12/11 1:59 PM

A Granddaughter, on her birthday,

promises that she will not puke,

well, at least until she is out of town.

Twenty minutes later,

she has given up the BBQ ribs,

the New Red Potatoes and creamed

green peas,

half a case of Bud Light-

Grandma's fresh baked buns!

Aunt Casey's shrimp salad!

All I wanted to eat

the next day,

they took home for samples,

dead plates, in the water and soap,

Why am I always the stupid one?

The one not smart enough to know,

that all she does serves her purpose,

and in the dark stands me, the dope?

Out of the herd that came,

a Grandson - with a book!

When asked if, who was the

writer of word

that turned his crank

and spun his wheels?

I laughed as he handed me the

pages from his soul and my heart.

Written by a man named, James Wright!

But what was so funny?

These are the words read,

every time I sit to shit!

Look up on the wall, while on the

porcelain throne,

let my belly unload, and

listen for the splash.

I read these words,

"Friends are the flowers

that bloom in Life's garden!"

Let's go smoke some hash.

Of course I cannot do that!

I owe a debt to all who come

after me,

'Do no harm, touch a heart or a soul

just to let them know-- it is always darkest,

before it is totally black!

Or just before you turn the

fucking light on!'

So into the 'Library', where I sit and rest,

I dump out all of the day's waste.

For all I need to do is read,

the words on the wall---

just to have a small taste!

So I sit and stink

while the day ahead

runs through the

process.

Ker Plop, Ker Plop!

There goes my brain.

Nothing left but truth,

honesty, and integrity!

What do I do with this information?

Will I tell,

ruin a small adult's reputation?

I am a liar, and a cheat,

if this gets glued on my

family, what kind of food

do I eat?

Bitter words of what I should have done?

Who needs dead?

Who needs just a small word?

After all the dust has settled,

did I do wrong? Did I mettle?

<u>see what your Father says after he reads this</u>

Sent: Tue 6/13/11 1:56 AM

It was my birthday, and on my bed

Lay a *Colt Frontier scout .22.*

To the south I walked, out of town

until all that was in front of me,

was miles and miles of sagebrush.

To most it would seem, barren,

and without life.

I knew better, this was full prairie,

Full of life, all kinds of life! All kinds

of things that to me,

were only targets!

For just five dollars, a case of 500

.22 shells,

just what the Colt needed for food,

and I understood!

Into the sage and creosote brush

I walked happily and eagerly,

full of the need to play

with my new toy,

while death followed

with great need.

Too dumb to know,

but the trigger got pulled,

six hollow points do

fill the cylinder,

six hollow points.

A blizzard hard had blowed

40 to 60 below zero!

When the wind broke,

I stepped into calm,

T- shirt was all I wore,

and the day was more

than I could have wished for!

I was all alone, gun in hand,

with the need to learn.

Could I be my own task master?

Would I be true to what

I wanted to be?

This was secret shit no one

would ever know-

this was secret shit

to me!

The town is at least a mile and a half

to my rear,

thirty miles to the south, forty to

both east and west

and I walked with no fear!

No one to watch me, no one to see,

no one who could say,

Don't do that!

A kangaroo rat jumped

into the fangs of the

wiggly that goes ssssss.

He struck, I shot,

the rat got away

and he told lies,

that would do all

of us proud!

He told of when the only

God we know for sure is

death, but he got away

and like most of us,

He lied!

I was too smart for

that cocksucker

a Colt will bring

him to his knees,

even if it takes another

forty grain, hollow point!!

No one knows but me of

how I learned to shoot-

I used all for my targets,

terrible things.

If you are loved enough,

will I tell you the hard earned

truths of life?

Even if you don't shoot,

never forget,

I taught your uncles to shoot,

your dad taught me how to hunt!

A hard half a month all of us endured,

heavy rain, tight money, we still tried

to just pay the day's cost!

At eighty miles an hour so we get

to Shelby, due south

but shit is about to happen;

fucking dead, chunks, legs-parts is parts!!

Mule deer everywhere!

Bits and parts!

We came through that

and missed the meal

in Shelby!

Your Dad looked at me

And I had no answer.

A .220 Swift will build all

kinds of lies!!

Heavy skies, dark blue,

a lot of water in them,

everything alive,

plant, crop and

targets!

All were seeking cover:

only an empty belly

would force

you into this-

weather so bad, if you

talked about it, you would

be lying!

Late for supper, but there

under a barb wire fence,

soaked to the bone,

stood a wet assed coyote!

The swift spoke again,

to my dying day, the look

on its face said ,"fuck you!"

Yuppers!!!

Then I put a replacement

shell in the rifle.

Not a word was said

about this for thirty years:

then I got drunk and

spilled the beans.

What could I say?

no glory in the facts,

no honor in the do'eth,

not much fun in telling

anything but the truth.

But to do so, would be

boasting, as I know

how fucking lucky it is to

do what I've done.

What has been seen,

has been done-

are you able to

make up something

Like this??

The real truth of this

Is in the memories,

In the learning,

In the doing!

But most of all,

In the telling!

The next day,

our nation wept

with the news,

JFK is lost.

A bullet has

taken away,

the joy of having

the thing that

is fun- gone.

Jagged and torn,

every soul and

and gentle newborn,

and all my thoughts,

"Bad idea,

not bad gun."

And the world goes flat again.

Someone has a new

plan, not for them,

but only for you!

RE: Rants and raving
Sent: 6/14/11 1:20 AM

Hi,

Since I have not heard

from you in a long time,

after begging to read

your words,

still nothing for me

to do -

like counting shit

from the birds!

A small plop is the sound,

my heart breaks,

while my tears match

each bird's shit,

and still no words

and then higher go the

stakes!

If you send the sounds of letters,

I will not shoot the fucking computer!

I am not so sure about you,

as you are far behind the

other suitor!

RE: Rants and raving
Sent: 6/14/2011 1:56 AM

Hi,

I'm sorry I have been away

for such a long fucking time

but no matter what

I know

that you know

that I'm thinking of you

I would rhyme to patch

the tears of anticipation

that I have torn

into the last week of your life

but I'm incapable

of sitting down with 5 minutes to myself

yet I sit and marinade myself in rage

the time ticks as I become only more and more pissed

sweat making fast lanes down my face

my heard pounds

and as I sit back and listen to the music played

I'm satisfied

and mumbling your lyrics along-

fits hand in hand

but this is an accomplishment

that you will never know

because in your computer

there is a bullet hole

sorry I made you wait so long

don't shoot next time

RE: Rants and raving
Sent: 6/14/11 2:48 AM

It is a sad fucking day when the only

way I have time with you,

is in a bad email.

My faults shout out loud,

your scream bounces

off of the stop sign at

the end of the street.

and your walls!

Too tight are the chains

that bind us.

No time to be together

and just create our fun.

Their ideas keep both of

you and me inside

their narrow minds!

And still I don't play with

a gun.

But a fucked up email I

will send!

Full of bullshit that I just made

up!

Or a look into my soul?

To touch your heart and core,

and backwards do I bend.

Forbidden for me to be,

was my first commandment!

Fear that I will corrupt is

a fart in the wind--

gone in a whiff of air,

smells real bad,

but like a bad thought

well sent ,

is just another idea gone

with nothing solid

nothing lent!

Sleep well, sleep sound,

you found your fucking laptop.

All I want is more and

then to find out, that all you want

is for me not to stop.

I do pretty good under a lot of

pressure and weight,

but this is way more

hard for me to swallow

as for your words I await.

Gordon Lightfoot sang

"Does anyone know where the

love of God goes when the

waves turn the minutes into

hours?"

So I wait to read,

or hear your voice.

another care package Hahahaaa
Sent: Tue 6/14/11 3:35 AM

A belly full of beer,

and inside my skin,

I accept the strong truth.

You sent me love,

with your words,

and I am a shit,

'uncouth!',

is not fair.

Your bag is not full of shit.

mine is, and I try

every day to empty it.

But just like trying to fly,

by flapping my arms fast enough;

I don't move and my words

mean the same thing!

We out of life take, and

grab our little bit!

That you and I

make a union

threatens all!

It is open war!

I still do not know why!

Maybe we were lost

and did not know.

What did we do?

Who did we threaten?

Should I care?

Or just sit and drink

my beer?

Contended, but

only if I dare?

Who will tell, who

will stare,

who's ass will be bare?

None with the courage

to walk a narrow path,

alone or together, through

bumps, rocks, and other

pains?

A look into us,

will show both of us will be,

rolled under the bus.

Into the ground, at

one time for each.

Time will stop the

both of us.

ten verses, and your mail box is full??fuck fuck fuck!!!!
Sent: 6/15/11 2:08 AM

To say that I take pen in hand,

is bullshit.

To have your words come to me,

I peck and search for the

right keys,

hoping that I find the

combination that sends

your thoughts back to me.

But is seems that I am not a

Soothsayer!

A wizard I am not-

but I did win the lottery last

year,

as I recovered six dollars

from what I spent!

And still I pray for just one night,

spent in the dark outside:

Fire working, stars are bright,

wood talks in embers red,

lies from me will pour,

mixed with enough truth

for the words to bring smiles,

as you head for bed.

Words from my past

and thoughts of you,

will show my love

as dreams often do!

So I fire the pipe and smile inside,

my soul laid bare,

with nothing to hide.

You give me unconditional love,

no price to pay, no toll to take,

just the history of what

my path has been.

Like when you took

your first deer,

in timber dark,

not one of me

did a sin!

That moment lives in

memories,

a picture in a frame,

so I don't forget,

what for me did seem as déjà vu,

success just the same!

Someone who loved me,

who was there,

when growth happened,

into manhood, standing bare!

The rite of passage you have

crossed-

just for you with loved ones,

with nothing lost!

Meat was made for supper, up soon

feels like dancing under the moon.

You did well, you did good.

Your Father and I both

knew, manhood faced you

where you stood.

childhood left you,

where you stood.

Making meat, soon to eat,

on a mountain, in dark wood!

Nothing left in life will come

near to the growth you made,

when you were responsible

for the death of supper,

with this deer!

The heart fried in bacon grease,

rolled in flour,

crisp and sweet

paid for my first grandsons

as they grew into men.

I would march into battle

with both of them!

RE: this is about the email in front of this one!

Sent: 6/15/11 3:07 AM

Now you have touched me,

and moved me like a stone.

My eyes leak, warm is my heart

and soul.

Walk anything close to the path

in back of me,

after all I've done.

to help raise the

little ones, and

share a slice of my soul.

I still love you, no matter

what they all think of me!

Stand tall and stand fast,

nothing will fix the battles

of the past.

Do better, do worse, in the long

run it will not matter,

but drunk or stoned,

none could have stood the test

that I faced alone!

tonight! revise a bit,now read --- let me know-

Sent: 6/17/11 2:47 AM

Hi t, I wanted to sit down and write

something that would matter

so of course, my head and heart

are burnt to a crisp.

All of my thoughts and

my heart, go all over,

and they are in a splatter.

Tonight, I worked a major softball game,

the only blue shirt on the field.

Fully wet from all the rain,

with nothing for a shield.

My skin is wet and cold,

my insides are soft and warm.

A terrific game with some good plays,

and some with lots of harm!

Even at this late hour,

of this very day

for me a job well done,

all by myself,

and I have nothing to say!

Someday soon, you should see,

what I do and what I give away!

What I did was not hard to do,

show up, do my best, and then

to go away.

A break in the game,

I spoke to the "Book",

"What is the score?

I want to know."

These are the words

out of me,

"What a game!"

Each team has gone to sleep,

woken up, and scored some runs!

Four or five times for each!

All outside the fence laughed

at that.

I went and brushed the plate,

got soaked in the rain.

Reached out a little bit,

touched the catcher on her

helmet.

Smiled a smile, and gently said,

'Great work!

After the next pitch, call two more,

and we'll see what happens?!

Ok?

So we played the full game,

and we all bump a closed fist.

"Good game! You really played well!

Listen to your Mom and Dad.

Try to do what your Coach

wants you to do!"

What a good game for all to see.

I still cannot believe they let me

on the Field.

When I go home, I know that

I have had more fun,

than half of the Ladies

who played this game!

Why do I do it?

I do it for free!

A strange gift comes

to those who volunteer,

those who do not,

just disappear!

Even the winning team

watches half of the game

through a wire fence!

While they sit in the dugout!

I work the game from the

behind the plate,

those outside the wire

have no defense!

Why don't they step up

and be a part of the solution?

Instead of being the ignorant parent,

who thinks they can make a difference?

Just pissing in the dark??

where are you now?

Sent: 6/21/11 1:44 AM

Hi,

you are gone and yet I want to

sit here full of selfishness,

talk with you, to hear of your day,

share a word or feeling,

or witty word.

With you gone,

my day is Less.

You sit in the bus to a foreign state,

with your lady love and yet you ride!

Like sitting with a bare ass on a

hard cactus!

No valuable place to hide!

It really is worse than having

a Hot Vick's enema!

No matter what the fuck,

you can't wait until it is over

and still you cannot figure out

how you earned this or what you

have done!

So goes the secrets of life,

some lessons come easy,

some come cheap,

But none come like a picture

on YouTube,

of you fucking a sheep-

no matter what, doesn't leave

a good image behind!

Oh yea! that is what it is about,

do no harm, treat all alike

look for gold in the heart of the

people you meet,

 a soulmate for you to find!

My uncle told me when he

pointed at a small pile of chicken shit,

"Just like most people and the words they say,

is just like that little white spot on top of that pile!'

Do you know what that is?"

"No," I said.

He laughed as he told me, "Just more chicken shit!"

So I sit here in the middle of the night,

needing to peck the keys,

needing to send a slice of my heart to you,

but home you are not, and these words you

will not see.

As it should be, you are on your way,

down your life path and hers!

No one will love you like this again,

on this trip, or ever!

Now all of this means you owe a fee,

to be paid for the love she freely gives!

Are we talking about your Honor?

Or about how your choices,

twist your lives?

Now if this causes some discomfort,

for you to feel

about how to conduct yourself,

you should know that a couple of

hard drop-kicks to the nuts,

will bring you back to life,

and to the shit hole we all wade through,

as we do,

what we do

for those we love,

and the hard times we face.

Sometimes the choice is easy.

Sometimes, it gets hard,

and that is when you will know

if you have done right,

do you discard?

Do you draw another card?

Do you earn your honor?

Time will tell you after you have

chosen poorly-

the divorce lawyers have your money,

the Judge has your honey!

Your bank account will suffer and

your ass will feel sorely!

So we all learn, that what we want now,

will hurt in the end, and

it matters not if our path was

straight, or had a bend!

But with the love of the one

beside you,

you will go through, and do things

that legends are made of!

And your generations to follow

will talk and tell lies about you.

So on to future day's battle fields,

we all walk into the unknown.

What will happen, what will be shown?

It matters not, what are our options!

Or do I just show to the one who loves

Me just how much she guides me,

as I walk through life with her??!!

I was here, but you were gone!

now you are here,

and I am gone!

The only evidence being

An unusual and empty smell

of belly gas turned loose

in a heavy breeze.

<u>early Monday morning!</u>

Sent: Mon 6/27/11 2:04 AM

Hi t, it takes a long time for you to be gone,

for another five days or so.

What the hell am I supposed to do,

to pass this time, while down the

road you and your lover roll?

Montana is a small bit of empty,

while you are in a foreign state!

Will you answer your phone,

or is it full?

Why do I have to wait?

I worked the Senior Babe Ruth games,

all of this last weekend.

The fun I had was a lot more than

all the teams had, except just one.

The team from here, played

well,

sent all the other teams,

away.

Two no-hitters, in a row, is what

the pitchers threw!

What more can I say?

So out-matched by the team from here,

who had all the fun.

At the end of the first inning, they

lead by twenty one!

The hard part was closing the game,

no one needs to be humiliated!

To show how much fun they had,

with the batted ball to the back fence,

they only took one base.

Looked at their manager,

shrugged their shoulders,

and stood their place!

A lot of class was shown today,

buy a team that is too strong.

They still had a ton of fun,

and none of it was wrong!

I called all kinds of shit,

way outside the zone.

To me it felt like there I was,

naked, vulnerable, and alone!

But not one person made a sound,

They knew what needed done.

The crew and me did needed

work,

we walked off the field as one.

I had no way to tell the crowd,

that none of this was fun.

Even the winning team,

smiled as I called them out:

All wanted this game done!

Over matched, and really out played,

they all came together.

They shook each other's hands,

bumped their fists,

and smiled,

nothing could be better.

<u>here you go with this one!</u>

Sent: Sat 7/02/11 11:06 PM

The creek rushed past at a strong rate,

not wide, not straight.

The fragrance of trout drifted off the water

of a live creek, with fish, and

I could smell it!

I picked a Tomas Cyclone,

Hammered brass, and opened

a small blister pack.

Fixed it to the swivel,

It looked like a Sculpin!

The perfect trout snack!

This was a meal, no trout

could pass up.

To me it would have seemed

like a big rib steak,

with fries and toast,

as it drifted by

working it's magic, wiggle wiggle,

impossible to not be eaten.

No need to beat the water

to a froth,

this lure could not be beaten!

Fried trout in the pan,

dishes on the table

waiting to be filled with spuds,

veggies and the taste of fables.

The angles in heaven,

weep large tears,

no fish will they taste.

We dine on our meal,

bones to the side

and nothing goes to waste!

The fire has burned down,

the coffee is in the pot.

All our girls are in their

bags, inside their tent

and now the coffee is hot.

I stirred the fire,

Rake1d the coals,

moved the pot..

all was right with me.

My wife is sitting here

beside me,

when from a nearby tent we hear,

"Look at that, Shelly!

There's dad fucking with

The fire!"

<u>making meat</u>

Sent: 7/08/11 4:41 AM

I stepped out of my blazer

4 wheel drive,

and we needed it.

The sky was perfect,

dark purple, even color,

and the wet came out;

Too hard to be called a mist,

not enough to be rain

but for the love of God,

it was wet!

I wore my wool,

top and bottom

insulation under all

of what I had on.

Within four or five minutes

out of the Blazer,

water ran down my arms

onto my rifle!

It had a heavy, loving

layer of carnauba wax,

the stock would not

take on water,

protected to the max!

The metal would not

take on rust,

I had no fear of it

getting wet

I was thankful

the sky said, "No Dust!"

On my feet were 'Danner,'

logging boots.

they cost a week and

a half of wages.

So I stepped into the dark timber.

All of home, work,

bills, and ass aches,

drifted away .

All that lay before me

was steep, and hard

country to hunt.

Of course, I came on

an old man and his woman

doing the old man chicken steps,

walking up the same trail I

was traveling on.

I spoke to them

and said, "I am sorry to mess up your hunt,

but I need to get another mile before I start

to side-hill."

"What are you after?"

was what the man with

the 'thurtty thurtty," said.

"I'm going to

kill an elk, and get

the meat out before dark!

I have to be at the sawmill

in the morning, to do my work,

earn a wage, or whatever, to feed

all who sit at my table.

I have to try to do this before dark."

A meal,

never dull or stark!

"Give me five minutes, and everything will move again.

I am so sorry for interrupting your hunt."

Ten minutes later,

I smell elk!

So I stepped off of the trail,

to my right,

took no more than ten strides,

and a calf elk stood up

from its bed

and committed suicide!

The heart and liver where inside a plastic bag-

If I pull this off, Supper!

Half of the meat made,

carried on my shoulders.

No! There is the old man and his woman,

doing the old man chicken steps,

coming up the trail.

early morning bullshit

Sent: 7/08/11 5:36 AM

I open up a new email and I freeze

what in the hell can I write about

that I haven't touched on already?

questions and sometimes answers zip through me

and the outside warm and rain-coated air soothes me

yet I just can't decide

just exactly what is in my mind

take one and you can talk to Jesus

take two and he will talk right back

and just beyond the line of sight

leaves me wondering, and wondering

so I take a seat at 12

blink my eyes and its fucking 4!

and the clock ticks again,

after yet another tick

and I sit

knuckles crack -

itch

Awww

Sent: 7/16/11 8:12 PM

You beg for words,

I long to tell.

You say you long for them,

I squeeze 'em from

hell.

But the night comes

and I want to talk to you.

I do my best, like a kitten,

to meet your needs.

I show my ass, nothing else to do,

but like a fool, who never sees;

your fucking mailbox is full!

And you don't read what is written.

No more shit will I send,

until you beg for more,

now my fucking computer is full-

like a two dollar whore!

<u>you did not see this one coming at you!! 1st draft?!</u>

Sent: 7/17/11 12:27 AM

What are you going to do?

How do you do this?

How do you eat?

Where are you going?

Questions poured out of me-

he might know!

I didn't know anything

after the last ten days,

but here was a kid, my age,

and he ran!

He ran up the mountain,

steep and terrible ground.

No way could I understand,

the knowledge he had found!

He had the courage to be

what I could not.

I wanted it, but I couldn't see.

He was small, just a snot,

but he showed he had the strength to do

what I had never thought of,

just leave!

Ran, which is 100 times faster that run!

So what now? What about tomorrow?

This banged in my head,

I had no chance to do this,

my belly empty,

my body cold.

I had no idea of where to

go after the top of the mountain.

Fucked from birth, cursed to

only failure.

What the hell do I do now?

What the fuck was he going to do?

I wanted to know!

I had no plan for this kind of shit!

At home, I knew how to dodge a

hard blow, and never take the

full force of the hit.

My sisters were in peril,

much smaller than me.

Too scared to see,

and watch as my small sisters

take my blows!

Too much a coward,

if only in my skin

I was there last year

now I only know how to run.

To my dying day, I regret

that I did not know how

to be far from the hive,

and just not be

but such are the fears

of the coward, when the school

bus pulls up at what is home.

Nothing but fear awaits me,

if you don't count what has happened.

I stepped out of the bus,

the front door has cardboard

over what used to be a window.

"Oh God, don't let any know,

don't let them see?"

I pleaded.

My belly turned to water,

I don't want to go,

and I don't want to be.

But forward was the only

thing to do, just like always.

I am afraid of inside home,

of what I will see!

Glass, windows, dishes,

the shit over the pictures.

Garbage, used as a weapon,

or maybe just a tool!

Filled every floor, and

room.

It don't matter, it will be

a long weekend!

Hell will hit real soon.

Time to run, time to be

the big coward.

Nothing I could do, for the little

ones.

If I don't freeze, just stay warm

tonight, wait for the morning sun,

see Mother's eyes, then know

if today is ok,

or now is the time to really run!

Not knowing ate at me like

a bear on a good kill.

Quitting was never my option,

In the morning I would be here

still!

Too young and dumb

to know anything but to

still be.

I knew, I never would tell,

that the coward,

was just me.

I stand here before all who

Have no idea of what hell is really like.

With a head held high,

nowhere to run,

nowhere to go,

not making a sound

until life is done.

shit, only eight verses this time-- what the fuck will you show me?

Sent: 7/20/11 1:56 AM

While sitting with a friend,

I talked of where,

at one time,

I had been.

I had a belly full of 'Cold Smoke' Ale,

I shared with no duress, in all of me.

The problem was,

while this went down,

my eyes leaked, and others thought

I was not worthy of being proud.

My therapist claims that it is

my grieving process!

Thank God he has his education!

I was surprised he told me this,

my harm was tears from my eyes.

So that night when I lay to sleep,

my bag of shit was not mine to keep.

Turn it loose, let it be,

the gift of this,

you will see.

The day will come when you

talk of this,

will not bring pain,

but only bliss.

It matters not what others think,

but only what I do.

Until they have walked my path,

in my shoes,

and let them tell 'truths'

of this gift, freely given

from me to all who's lives,

have touched my soul.

I still Pray today, that none

of them or theirs, come close

to being like a foal,

who faces life with no control.

I go through each day,

and I try to never sin.

Only to look for comfort,

for my heart and soul,

as I seek forgiveness inside my

skin.

aww, this is bad!

Sent: 7/20/11 10:36 AM

Early Wednesday I open my email with anticipation,

about the crack of noon

but of course your fucking phone is full

and I feel the weight of doom.

When I get my hands on you,

we are going to roll around on

the ground, just like before,

and punch each other

in the face

until our arms

are sore.

Another work

Sent: 7/22/11 5:55 PM

Being young and stupid,

without common sense.

A hunger for a belly full of beer,

and a need to shoot pool.

Only wanting fun

and willing to pay to have

no defense,

I walked into the King of

27th street's bar in Billings.

His name was skittle's,

giggles, or something like that.

He had shot the other pimp in

the head.

On the sidewalk, in front of all the watchers,

He shot the pimp dead!

The dead pimp, bad-mouthed the

wrong man, I suppose.

Two bullets from a 38,

left one man dead-

With the shooter to be

the only one to still stand,

after all was said.

So of course, I wanted to see,

could I walk amongst strong men.

Just to drink beer, shot pool,

have some laughs,

make some jokes,

and all will see.

Some say I was stupid,

some say I was a drunk

but those who say these words,

have no balls, no hope

and they leave an odor

like a road killed skunk.

The balls roll crazy and the balls

roll true.

It happens to all who play this game

of drinking beer and shooting pool!

The killer pimp lost ten bucks or so,

I bought ten pitchers,

in a row!

Grinned my dumb ass smile,

stroked the cue, sunk the

money ball.

"Drink up my friends.

this pitcher is on me!" I said.

"My babies sleep at my home,

my wife is waiting just for me.

I will pay for this night of fun,

long past when time will tell."

what I ask is where's my sin?

Shooting pool, or drinking beer?"

Am I gone, or am I here?"

Asdkfjio
Sent: 7/22/11 6:50 PM

You have to learn how

to do this shit

and still work all day.

All the time you rest your guts,

will prove that you are an asshole,

or just nuts!

Do you have your little hair curlers,

all in their place?

On your feet the fluu fluu slippers?

Do you take up needless space?

Your fucking mail box is full!

Fuck all who have a voicemail box full!!

Don't want to talk, or even see

The one who loves them!

Fuck it, I may not be!

Re: wwwwwhere are you?

Sent: 9/13/11 2:36 AM

The sun climbed the horizon, giving life to the prairie grass that moved with the warming air as the antelope came awake. Miles of eastern Montana came alive with the scent of sagebrush, creosote brush, and grass; Life for all that lived here in Heaven, small and large - all of us!

Small grasshoppers came alive as the dark breaks and leaves. The sun sets fire to the prairie grasses. The air looked like it could have been in a painting- but it kept moving , slowly, but steady! All of the ground for a mile wide, four miles long, slowly moved, undulating as a living, life-breathing thing, steady and sure-as-hell, hot. Life caressed this entire valley!

I held the custom built .257 Weatherby gently as I moved behind a small ridge, only a foot or two above the level ground that looks like it is flat as it lays at the bottom of this basin. It is many things, but it is not flat! Now this is the fact: there is not a flat hundred foot chunk of ground suitable for a football field in the eastern half of Montana. I still crawled on my hands and knees, through the prickly pear cactus, and all of the rest of the thorns and shit that will take its toll, a small price to pay to make winter meat. Under the barb wire fence-soon my toy will bark, and winter meat is made this way in my part of Heaven, where I hunt and live now.

This rifle was a terrible weapon-- cable of turning a jackrabbit into something you could not see, and as the trigger broke, it just disappeared in front of your eyes, even if you were the one looking through the scope- three hundred and fifty yards away, instant mist!

From the point of impact, just parts is parts, going back forty feet, nothing left for supper!! It spit out a hundred grain bullet at over 3700 hundred feet a second; flat shooting, deadly on the receiving end!

Re: more bullshit

Sent: 9/13/11 11:29 AM

Nobody wants to hear my story

I continuously peruse

unless you're a fuck head,

you'll believe it's true!

On a day when the rain

could not have been more intense

I was humping through the woods

and sneaking over fence.

Hours I had wasted

patiently awaiting

and listening for

a 5 point mule buck

I spent all my money

buying camouflage

and borrowed some coins

to buy some urine scent

I researched for hours

and heard all over town

of where the best hunting was

but promised to keep it on the low down

I awoke at 4

thirty minutes before dawn

with excitement in my belly

knowing soon I would be gone

I packed my truck

with a cooler and ice

and snacks,

for dragging out a trophy

would surely provoke an appetite!

I drove to the secret place

and exited my truck

flung my Ruger over my shoulder

and through thicket,

I quietly snuck

I thought I had caught a scent

of a rutting bull elk

but it soon passed-

I continued on my way

I came across a doe

with a fawn in tow

which could have filled my freezer

but, no

hours passed

sweat dripped down my ass

I was getting pissed

'Fuck it' I thought

So I pulled out a smoke,

unfiltered,

put fire to it

and inhaled

that seemed to help

by now it was nearing dusk

just as always, my day held no luck

I walked for an hour

back to my truck in the dark

pissed. Just pissed!

On my way home

I stopped at a convenience store

to buy some beef jerky

and maybe a cheap whore

Again with no luck

I proceeded down the highway

and turned on Johnny cash

and sang along lightly

with eye lids

like cement walls

Barely awake, I pulled into my driveway

where I took a second take

so quick I kinked my neck

at the bedded 6 point under the hedge

<u>3:27 AM</u>
Sent: 9/17/11 3:41 AM

So blessed am I

when you touch my soul, and heart.

the minutes together

are worth more

than millions of desired $'s!

For me, I see you having a

part time job walking people's fish!

Your new Nike's will be dry,

what will that taste like served

upon his supper dish?

Food stamps will not be an option for

you to know about or see.

No matter what happens to you or me,

with the education you are working on,

none of us are worried about how

you will be.

When you are an old man, you sit

next to one of your itty bitties,

love will fill your soul with warmth,

setting your heart on fire-

no matter what you have fucked up,

in the end, you will still stand tall.

Face all who attack, even if the

outcome seems dire!

What will Heaven be like tasted?

I am too lazy

to satisfy my own need to do well-

that means something of me given,

was not wasted!

<u>did you see this coming?</u>

Sent: 9/20/11 8:25 PM

Doors are locked,
turned off all the lights.

Your warm scent tells me,
I am getting your delights!
You reach for me, as I you,
hands hot as only lovers know!

Doors open upon fields unknown
passion for both of us unsown
worlds collide, heart's meld,
no longer are we???

From now--we are one.
Our hearts do one thing,
our bodies glue us together,
just to be!!

Now what the fuck do we do?

mother's day

Sent: 9/21/11 4:52 PM

Gram Frizzle, back from the mail box,

says, ' Just bills we can't pay!"

Aww shit, I forgot!

It's that time of month.

It's Mother's day!"

Money I have not!

This time of month women know,

because of the moon phase!

But to be Mother's day,

shows all I can do is

babble and bullshit,

none of them can I pay.

So on the 20th of each month,

I call it 'Mother's day!'

'Cause every Mother that has us,

at their beck and call,

think of us as indentured

servants, and they require all!'

So we face these monthly bills,

without holding our Lord's staff.

My ass slammed shut, tight enough,

to choke a railroad spike in half!

six short verses!

Sent: 9/22/11 2:47 PM

I wanted to write today, for you,

so I could show off.

Four fucking hours later,

I paid for lessons on playing golf!

Inside my skin, wages a war,

nothing comes out of my fingers.

A belly full of rot gut booze-

so I drink another full jigger!

A rewrite for me is not possible,

first I have to write some dribble!

Now six hours later, fully drunk,

I cannot even scribble!

For one so full of shit,

this should be really easy!

I show my ass today,

as now I get all dizzy!

I have not had a viable thought,

nothing I could use.

We all have to pay for lessons,

and now I pay my dues.

I will wad this shit all up,

and throw it in the waste bucket!

The best thing that I can do,

is back away as I say, "Fuck it!"

Oh,,God- Did I fuckup tonight! Now only five fucking verses!

Sent: 9/24/11 12:25 AM

With you not here tonight,

you can't believe what I've done!

I let your Mother, read our last words,

that passed between the both of us!

Now we both are in dire straits,

our nuts are on the fire!

Well, not yours, but for sure, mine!

And the flames burn higher!

Your Mother can't contain her giggle,

She says," Both of you, or one of you,

is nuts, and both of you are liars!

No one can hear what bangs inside your head,

you both walk many strange miles."

Well, when I hear these words,

all that kicks in for me, is pure fear!

Too much armor, I laid down,

so a grandson knows,

my soul, laid wide open,

no lies, no regrets, no tears.

If you are a wizard,

or you know what I should do,

tell me how to not have the itty bitties,

pay for my faults, as only the

innocents, have to do!

Thump-bingo-whomper!

when you are grey whiskered,

you will know--

The clock ticks for all of us,

only for the rich to know--

all of your money will not change the

the beat of the life clock!

if these words come to print-envious are those who read

Sent: 9/26/11 4:37 AM

In the heading tells all of our truths,

my reality has changed,

you own my heart!

There are no words to

make any of this be different,

the dark stares at me,

yours is just starting out.

If you have heard any of my words,

let life bathe all of the itty bitties,

in your life, give you the same rewards

all of you have given me.

You have to be willing to see,

don't let bitterness keep you company.

Instead, let the children help you understand,

your nuts are on the fire, does not mean

the stove needs twisted higher!

They are what we leave behind,

if I did my part.

I hold a small part of each of your hearts.

I pray you don't shit your pants,

only slip out, small empty farts?

If I am lucky, all of you will remember

only a small thing, I am the fat one that

loves you above all others!

In the dead of night, when I touch your soul,

rest easy, I only want you to know that you,

walk with all of us who lead you down this path.

It's our duty to show what you have to face ,

you do not walk alone, with your grace,

you give us purpose.

you cannot fault us for what we are bound

to do.

When your clock runs out,

you will do this too!!

yesterday- 46 years-- someone's anniversary

Sent: 9/28/11 2:44 AM

So sorry to hear you have the same shit as I,

But comes people with long years of being there.

Sick or not, most of our daughters, most of

the grand kids, with a few great grandchildren thrown in,

had a meal of fried chicken, gravy that melted in your mouth.

Mashed potatoes, and of course, cornbread!

Since you were not there, you did not hear the words said.

What the day was like, and the shit that followed,

the stories that were told, with both of us sitting there.

No one lied, no one stretched a single word.

46 years ago, we took all there, as we eat of this meal.

The Priest that married us, knew we were so broke,

we could not pay attention!

So instead of us paying him ten dollars, for all he did,

he gave us a twenty, as he said," The rhythm method doesn't

work, make her take the pill, you little jerk!"

Her older sister's husband had printed, on the

bottom of my 'go to church shoes.'

Polished up until they shined, but under the heel,

on the left one, in white shoe polish, in big print,

"Help".

On the right one, "Me!"

No one would see until we knelt for Communion,

before our union, of being man and wife.

As shit happens, we went through our ritual in the Church.

Safety lay were we did not know yet.

Seven miles driven to the reception, but more

excitement before we get there.

We were young, just married, what the fuck did we know?

Before a bite of farm, homemade buns, salads, fried chicken, and all of the other women thingies to eat, at something like this-

Her older brother says to me, "the Sheriff wants to see you,

before you leave!"

"Aww fuck! it's the toilet paper from there to here?" I yelped

"No. He has your papers. You've been drafted!"

3:00Am your mailbox is full

Sent: 10/01/11 3:23 AM

it is early in the morning,

I can't leave a message,

'cause your mailbox is full!

Of course I'm sick, no sleep,

no mail from you.

Dry heaves rack my soul,

no rest, no lifting of my head!

Not a word from you do I hear,

my heart is empty, so instead

of being pissed,

I turn into a wizard, send myself to bed.

I can't believe the shit I say,

to me, inside my skin, after the flu,

the words are not spoken, fuck you!

I know you are running on empty.

My vanity shows itself, and I go back,

to the center of the universe,

truly hard for me to see!

With no word from you,

back to bed, under quilts,

maybe sleep will come,

my ego may just wilt.

bullshit we have to go through

Sent: 10/06/11 3:47 AM

It has always amazed me,

of the bullshit we have to go through,

so we have a minute or two,

to do what we want to do!

But our obligations dictate and fragment

our time,

we are whores to what others want

our nuts are beaten flat.

It makes no difference if it hurts,

their wants make us land,

like bird shit, Ker-splat!

So we jump into hoops and

when we land,

we look around,

just to see if this time

we understand!

I waited for a certain age,

so I could have a say,

in how my day would go.

When boiled down,

not a word from me,

as their drumbeat told me so.

When the fuck do I get to do

exactly what I want to do?

Oh! When I want to do it?

Shit! I am back to being the

center of the universe...

it is a lonely place.

No room for anyone else,

it is such a small space.

How do I recover when

there is egg all over my face?

<u>here is one of the fucking rewrites-publishable--what do you
think? gpa</u>

Sent: 10/11/11 3:45 AM

Just going to the University

will open doors for you.

Things will become available,

If, you buy into all of the worthless bullshit.

You will need to do research;

the Library will not be a friend!

A priceless hunk of shit will

have all the reference books

checked out!

Only, it is you

that pays in the end.

But at the end of four years

all of the needless shit

you will be forced to eat

will make your brain rattle.

But you will have a piece

of paper that proves,

you did not quit.

It is a Badge of Battle!

are you up now?

Sent: 10/12/11 11:50 PM

I was here,

but you were gone.

Now you are here,

and I am gone!

<u>If it tastes good, spit it out!</u>

Sent: 10/16/11 6:01 PM

I was feeling real poorly

I sniveled all the time

old age had crept up

on me, I'm not in my prime.

So grandma made me go see

the only one who thinks I have too

much money!

He ordered me to take all kinds

of tests!

I didn't think he was funny!

But the cholesterol numbers,

told a tale of eating

sweet Grandma's cooking

fried chicken in cream gravy!

Acorn squash soaked with hand

squeezed Amish butter!

Kosher salt on all of my meal.

Then came the words to

chill my soul;

"Nothing you eat now will keep

you out of a six foot hole!

But you can eat all the cardboard

you can choke down.

"Liver, all you can want!

Sauerkraut, by the bucket!

Anything else, if it tastes good,

spit it out!"

God!! I loved today!

Sent: 10/16/11 10:47 PM

God!! I loved today.

The ones held back from me,

two decades, and finally,

I get to see.

Two children alive with us,

not just me, but Grandma cried.

Just to watch all of you, having fun,

to warm our hearts, it was you we

sat beside.

A Junkie in the projects,

wants what he wants.

And he wants it now!

You made us laugh,

all of you,

We made you laugh with sound!

Not a word was spoken,

no one heard a harm.

Our bellies hurt from

all the giggles,

you made us laugh out loud!

'Deer Killer' went out our front door,

toy Rifle in his hands--

four years old,

making winter meat.

Of course we think he's grand--

we soon will have meat to eat!

Re: Hi t – keep this one on file

Sent: 10/18/11 2:32 PM

Hi t – tell your dad to call me - gpa

What's the reason for this world

Too often its people make me hurl

In sophistication people are kind

And it blows my brain from my mind

What's the secret of heaven earth and hell

All but childhood is a broken bell

And all you once achieved

Lives, dies, and leaves.

What's the point of living life in pain

Comparable to walking in the rain

Comforting and cold

And then you realize you've grown old

Re:

Sent: 11/23/11 10:47 AM

I teach the 8th grade

and it suits me fine.

But a nagging doubt

still haunts my mind.

It is about a boy

who walks like a king.

No matter the homework,

to him, it is nothing.

On Monday, I give this

week's assignments.

all must be done,

it comes with a test.

He sits at the center of my desk,

first in line, first in front of me.

When I look into his eyes,

that have age, wisdom, survival,

they tell me there is more to see.

He will ask for the test,

back to his seat.

He will do the test,

and talk to me.

Of course he aced the test,

and pulls out a book from the library.

He reads while I talk, aware of the class,

never too far away, his soul must be brass.

I really don't know what he reads,

I am afraid to look.

He has all his answers,

just from reading a book.

I want to know what it is like,

inside his skin!

Why does a child live with

the richest family in our town,

never hear, what is it like for him?

All who know him, but for a simple few,

ridiculed by some, ready to make a friend anew!

They all thought of him as a fool,

just failure, to be seen soon.

<u>next</u>

Sent: 11/24/11 1:57 AM

I tried to set him up,

I sprung a test, just for him.

He shook his head,

looked me in the eye.

"I thought better of you,

I thought you understood."

"I will talk to your paper,

maybe, if you could,

think of this as failure,

but in front of you I stood."

I looked at him, small, and

young.

I threw out the gauntlet.

I wanted his resolve.

His courage beside him, I was the fool.

This kid scared me, while he showed

where I failed.

He stepped into each second,

like a ship under sail.

How am I to deal with this,

no one is allowed inside.

No one the boy shows

his heart to,

will live and survive.

1st draft of a new song-- you did not see this one coming!

Sent: 12/01/11 1:56 PM

I've loved you from the first grade,

all the way through high school.

We giggled as we kissed,

God! We were so cool!

From the first second I saw you,

your inner beauty was a light.

Blinding like the glow that

comes,

from seeing an Angel, shining bright.

God! We were so cool!

You were the only one I danced with,

no one else could compare.

When we were together,

all stopped and they would stare.

God! We were so cool!

The day I bought a shiny thing,

the smile when you saw the ring.

What else could we do?

My heart was full!

God! We were so cool!

I was blinded by your light,

it came from Angel's souls.

That's when you started fucking

Other guys – even my cousin!

Now you look like a sack of busted

assholes.

God! Was I such a fool!

here is another path to trudge down,

Sent: 12/07/11 4:41 PM

Do you see the wide eraser

on your ass-end?

It leaves a wide trail,

just below where you bend.

It wipes out all your mistakes,

but it harms your vanity.

Kicks you in the nuts,

leaves you puking;

for all to see!

When the dust raises

above you ears,

blocks your eyes,

only a wizard knows,

what is the size?

No one is to blame,

you chose your path.

How much damage are

you willing to deal with?

Will it be God's will,

or Satan's path?

In the night you will ask,

what the fuck did I do to

command God's wrath?

Am I only young, dumb, and ignorant,

or could it be that I really know,

that I need to ask a question?

I just don't know what the fuck

to ask!

So fucked!!

What am I supposed to do?

Will it take an answer from a saint

or from a drunk?

Do we all have questions that come

hard?

Are the answers scattered like broken

glass shards?

What should I do? Where do I look?

Or can I make my fortune playing cards?

Not for me, no easy answers,

into the battle field I must march.

Soon we will see if my spine

is made of soft shit,

or has a harder core,

and maybe my backbone has

some starch.

But time will tell,

maybe, I will be full of

bullshit!

Selfish, self-serving,

without the courage to look

into the mirror of life,

what the fuck will I see?

My bowels make nothing but water,

how the fuck do I do this,

and not just shit myself?

Scared beyond nightmares,

How am I supposed to do this?

The one question that has haunted me!

If I am good, what about my revenge,

why do I wage war at night?

Where have I sinned, what ground

do I stand on,

to have this fight?

Enemies come and they all go.

Now where is the battle,

can you tell me?

Where is my next foe?

Fw: I needed to let this brew for awhile

Sent: 12/10/11 7:02 AM

I'm no different than you are,

we all have one in our family.

They make us look at them,

as they show a side we're not to see.

My uncle came to baby brothers birthday,

as he had just turned five.

He came in old Carharts,

wearing duct tape over the suspenders,

bungee cords around his waist,

with carpet layers knee pads!

What could we say, as we all took a look.

No one had the guts to ask, 'cept grandma!

"What the hell are you wearing knee pads for?"

Her eyes were filled with that look,

she was on top of it!

All of us had our asshole's slam shut,

tight enough to choke a railroad spike in half.

She was the one with courage to ask,

and the words that came out of fucked up uncle,

gave us cause to laugh.

"Well, I keep falling down on my knee pads."

"Ok," came from grandma.

"What are the bungee cords for?"

"They hold up my pants."

A soft look went around the room,

as we all knew,

crystal meth, or something worse!

God, we want to love him,

but he leaves us no choice.

He is too fucked up for us to hear,

what truly is his voice.

So we live with that hard news,

what more can we do?

He flops down on the floor,

just to show that he is the fool.

Just like a lot of families,

with one who breaks our hearts.

So how do we live with this,

as in his own hell he dances?

We watch him sink into dark,

there is nothing we can do.

When he is finally gone,

who do we sue?

We all have played this game,

and helped him down his path.

So how do we look into the mirror,

and stand, and still pay God's wrath?

<u>lets see what you make of this shit?!</u>

Sent: 12/13/11 3:26 AM

Three score and five years,

I sit up late at night.

I went down my path,

no regrets, none have had

to walk in my tracks.

Of course I'm drunk,

so fucking what?

Old, and afraid of nothing,

I am staring into the dark.

Maybe now, a glass pipe

of hemp,

what stings the most is

the little ones who will

not know--what was me.

The ones I know now, all

think I should have a spare job

walking people's fish.

And if I am not 'working',

it is game on, let's play!

Cluttered around my feet are

all the little rat bastards,

with a sparkle in their eyes-

no matter what; fun, no trouble,

no ass whipping,

"Cause the old fucker started it!!!"

Well, how the hell am I supposed to tell

about that, and still look great?

My body betrays me, with every breath,

my time is short, so fucking what?

It is my fate.

And all of the little pin heads,

can't wait until Sunday breakfast,

at the sweetest woman's table

with a fat man,

none thought would last.

But the fat man was fat for a fucking reason:

he could cook!

But Grandma was better

at everything except pancakes.

Now for breakfast, it was a loaded game.

Bacon, sausage, ham, an idiot can make that!

Grandma kept pissheads all in line

while pancakes were made,

by the man who was a little fat.

His family came together on Sunday morning,

for food!

Early, like the crack of noon.

They all would leave with

a full belly, and knowing,

next Sunday, pancakes!

I do wish my time was longer,

but I met a herd of great grandchildren,

We play fuck-fuck,

they will fuck with me,

I stir the shit pot and we all laugh

and none but them will see!

The itty bitties are so dear to my heart,

I wonder, will they see what they meant to me?

Only time will tell if I got any of this shit right,

their offspring will tell the tale,

and then they will be the ones who see!

I tried to call you,

since your mailbox is full

I will send this to,

and go to bed.

I pray this was not dull.

I did my part, showed a slice of

my soul.

While I look at the grave,

soon all will not see!

You are young, your plate is full,

just like me,

I am old, and my pants are full!

did you see this coming?

empty your fucking mailbox!!

I am looking at the grave!

<u>another avenue to take the first killer album-</u>

Sent: 12/14/11 3:43 PM

I watch the ocean's wash over you

there is nothing you can do.

A school bully comes at you

what else can you do?

You faced that chunk of shit,

kicked his ass.

Life or him could not turn,

you from your path,

he felt your wrath

God, I wanted to be a part of that,

then I could rest easy, in my skin.

Not to whoop up on him,

but to be there when you

answer for your sin.

The hard truth about our lives,

come harder for some,

than others.

No matter what is said,

we are loved, if only by

our mothers!

It is your turn to walk your path,

eat some shit, and see.

If you do this right,

all will be well,

and be who you will be

But if you fuck up,

the weight of what you carry,

will tell a tale of when you failed.

And that becomes real scary!

How the hell are you supposed to know,

right turn, left turn, or straight, should you go?

The painful truth of life, if we should know,

is when we fuck up, too late, too long,

and we reap only what we have sown!

A.W. JOHNSON

What do you think of rhea? feed back is needed

Sent: 12/17/11 12:59 AM

I sit here, thinking of what it means

to be sixty five?

Who would ever believe,

from the night that made

me want to survive,

util now, not knowing how.

In baby brother's cot,

with me,

the oldest of my younger sisters,

pissed around, for hours.

I knew the worst was coming.

Truly afraid to think, or see.

Scary were the last few days,

breaking glass, other stuff

ruined!!

To school three of us go.

We hear the kids talking

about the cardboard where

we one-time had a window.

Our time is up, off of the school bus.

Dread is not the word for what we all felt,

as we looked at each other, for sure,

No one had an invitation to a sleep-over:

not from us!

We go inside, baby sister is in her crib,

six weeks old.

She will never know, why all of us

have a belly full of puke.

We don't know why,

we don't care.

Just please, not one more

rebuke?

"Something has happened,

I don't think it is good."

It was like talking to a fence post.

No one heard, no one cared,

and then it got darker.

"No, really,,

things just changed!

I'm not sure how,

but now, everything is different."

We all think that our pastures will turn

greener.

Only for us, we had no chance,

the taste of life got leaner.

Our imagination, had not a valid

reference point.

It mattered not if we understood,

no wonder we now crave a joint!

stupid shit the itty bitty's say-you better call me when you read this shit!

Sent: 12/26/11 12:21 PM

Christmas Goose is golden brown,

monsters galore, from all over town.

Blessed, are all who come to see grandma,

or 'ggma'!

With bellies full, hearts warm

and tender,

we watch the monsters play.

Yea, I know, I'm getting to it,

inside every child lives a monster!

When they outgrow the monster,

they become adults!

What can we say?

So brand new toys are being played,

kids playing, just having fun.

We all are watching, and making smiles,

talking talk, and none want this day done.

Trey says to his Mother,

"Look Mom, I got the video of, 'The diarrhea of a

wimpy kid!'

We are in tears, we're laughing so hard.

We could not buy this, no matter how high we bid.

Dinner is done, now comes the suitcase!

old, from the 'long time ago!'

full of pictures, filled with memories,

we tell names, places, and who they

were!

The afternoon flows.

Out of nowhere comes a voice,

"Mom, I know God is black!"

"What? How do you know this?"

"Well Mom, when I close my eyes

to talk to him.

All I see is black!"

Someone please call 911!

I think I pissed my pants.

looking at the ne+xt week- do you want more?

Sent: 1/14/12 9:11 PM

I want to write the words tonight,

just the ones that will impress.

I kissed the end of a glass pipe,

run my lips around a glass.

I have not the courage to see,

what I look like, just to be.

A hard winter storm will hit

in an hour or two

behind the snowplow steering wheel,

at twenty hours in a stretch!

Finally I have a chance to

make money,

not be a total wretch.

Just do my part, move the snow.

When we are disposed,

I will know if what I do,

is worth all the grief.

I will never be rich,

only once a month do

I taste beef.

<u>here are five small verses === what do you think?</u>

Sent: 1/29/12 8:24 PM

I step into the morning sun,

into warm light, until it is done.

I walk into the shadows of

the afternoon,

Hell follows soon.

It matters not to me,

I really don't care.

I walked within my path,

you can slobber, drool, and stare.

No harm will come to me,

my soul is not spoiled.

I will work my ass off,

and I will sweat, while I toil.

I support three generations,

of little rat bastards.

The greatest gifts, been given,

to an old bat fastard!!

Of course it is warped and twisted,

what else do you expect?

No matter how fucked up we are,

they all bring us redemption!

<u>you won't talk to me--so here is five more- i know you did not see this one coming!!</u>

Sent: 1/30/12 10:54 PM

I sit here inside my skin,

go fuck yourself to do better.

I walk in all kinds of storms,

can you get much wetter?

The babies just want a touch,

so they know;

they are here not alone.

We all are here;

worthless, without power.

We all look like we are slow.

What do you do when the

bathroom mirror shows,

better could have been done.

The hard part is just seeing

me, who failed again,

and I am the only one.

The words that come out of my fingers,

feels soft and warm,

gives comfort.

Not like the dark alone, or cold deep dirt.

Just nothing else can hurt.

Do you look into the mirror,

or do you just dodge?

So what should I tell myself,

at night?

how do you like this one?

Sent: 02/01/12 3:08 PM

I don't know what to do,

when the dark covers me.

Where do I turn for help,

if only just to see.

Cold ground is not a fear for me,

what I need to know is how to

face the unknown--

not death, just ignorance of

what to do, fully grown.

It seems like being a parent,

is only learned by experience.

When that is gained, the harm is done,

for it's the young who pay the price,

when we stand in dark, waiting for the sun.

Did I do this right, or all wrong?

Marched down the easy path,

trying to do right,

but I still sang a song

with words I chose,

and a tune to play.

Years in the coming,

to hear the children say.

It matters not how you

fucked all this up.

You stood your ground,

and tried your best.

Now we see how we do,

on this second go-round.

We hope to hear the same sound,

of laughter, fun, and we hold our poise,

and each of us gain the right to hear such noise.

(No Subject)

Sent: 5/14/12 11:54 AM

Betrayed.

An old man loves me.

My secrets kept safe, with him,

even when his body betrays.

No so with him!

So why do I get a gift,

of someone who loves me.

One who will not betray,

who stands strong,

through a family rift?

So I have someone in my corner,

battle scared, worn weary, in pain.

But I come first!

What the fuck did I do?

What dragons did I slay?

Why is it just me loved so?

Who the fuck is this old man?

A gift given freely,

I didn't do anything.

He makes my heart,

just want to sing.

Unconditional love,

Not a game of fuck-fuck!

Betrayal comes easy to who we love,

it opens a chink in our armor.

Also shows a tender spot,

sink the ax deep!

An open doorway to my soul.

(No Subject)
Sent: 5/16/12 12:29 PM

The best part of me,

lives in my soul.

The other part lives inside

my skin.

How do I pay for

what I have done?

How do I make my

Amends?

How do I atone?

It matters not my

intentions!

Or, how hard I try.

I know what the bitter

truth is.

How do I face me,

inside my skin?

(No Subject)

Sent: 5/18/12 4:25 PM

Making a difference,

just being!

Who would know?

Who would see,

what they

were seeing?

Not you at the center,

it is too full.

The center of the universe,

is lonely, when you take

up all the space.

Just how do I fit in?

You spit out the north end

of a south bound bullshit raven bird-

just shit!

Go ahead and tell me again,

How do I make a difference?

Let's not tell lies, now is for

honest truths!

A stick in your eye

makes lies into truths!

Why don't you fix my needs,

tell me I make a difference?

Take all of me, and then

make your defense.

Just to make a difference,

in my life- would be nice in

your heart- maybe in your soul.

<u>some times I fart in school</u>
Sent: 5/24/12 7:11 PM

Who could have known,

who would have said,

prison was not my destiny.

But a little piss head that

tells me:

"Sometimes in school I fart!"

"What?"

"Ya, I do! and everyone there

says it smells like poo!"

Four years old, full of

piss and vinegar!

Not afraid to tell me,

that he plans to go far!

His face I carry to the grave.

My Mother and Father's faces forgotten,

lost to time.

But this little rat bastard owns my heart!

Each minute with him is fine!

And he says, "Yea, I do! I really do!"

The twinkle in his eyes tells me that to him,

it is ok to fart in school.

He can tell me, and it is funny-

to both of us!

No one can take that away.

But when you have too much air inside,

and it comes out, no one wants the smell

of poo!

But to him, it is way too funny.

I can't make this up!

It could make us both dead;

I give him a huggy roll squeeze,

and a soft tussle to his head!

He turned easy into the light,

a chunk of licorice.

Just a soft word to let him know,

how it turns out will not be known,

But hot and sour soup is just his dish

It is not a game of luck against luck,

it's just both of us having fun.

If you know me, is it too greedy

to love him like the next breath of air?

Here I stand, right or fair- For him to be.

He won't see it, but the game has been on for some time now!

D&Q-- you should see the first part! ----call me gpa

Sent: 6/05/12 1:07 AM

Who knows when a caress there,

a soft touch here,

turns the night into the last chance,

for both of us, just you and me.

A softness in your eyes,

from the moment I saw you.

I just stood and stared as dreams

fed my fantasies, but it

turned yours into a nightmare!

Your hard body, green eyes,

I was harpooned and lost-

never thought you would be mine!

A hard battle fought with

a huge cost!

Our nights now, where we've grown old

Still, for each other, our loves are warm.

Heart soft and your soul full.

My love will cause no harm.

ABOUT THE AUTHOR

Read from page 1.

Made in the USA
Las Vegas, NV
15 December 2020